SHADOW CATS
The Black Panthers of North America

Michael Mayes

Anomalist Books
*San Antonio * Charlottesville*

An Original Publication of ANOMALIST BOOKS
Shadow Cats: The Black Panthers of North America
Copyright 2018 by Michael Mayes
ISBN: 978-1938398902

Cover Photo: Karen Fory
Book Design: Seale Studios

All rights reserved, including the right to reproduce this
Book or portions thereof in any form whatsoever

Every attempt has been made to find and contact all copyright owners of the photos used in this book. We would be pleased to hear from any copyright holders who have not been properly acknowledged in the book for correction in future editions.

For more information about the author,
visit www.texascryptidhunter.blogspot.com

For information about the publisher, go to AnomalistBooks.com, or write to:
Anomalist Books, 5150 Broadway #108, San Antonio, TX 78209

For Amanda Ward:

No one deserves an answer to this mystery more than you.

Contents

Foreword by Dr. Angelo Capparella vi
Author's Note ix
Preface xii
Introduction xiv
Chapter 1 – A Matter of Semantics 1
Chapter 2 – Historical Accounts and Folklore 6
Chapter 3 – Contemporary Black Panther Accounts 14
Chapter 4 – Is There Enough Suitable Habitat? 32
Chapter 5 – Zeroing In 44
Chapter 6 – The Suspects: Jaguar 51
Chapter 7 – The Suspects: Cougar 65
Chapter 8 – The Suspects: Jaguarundi 75
Chapter 9 – The Suspects: Giant Feral Cats 86
Chapter 10 – The Suspects: Escaped Exotics 96
Chapter 11 – The Science Behind Melanism 108
Chapter 12 – Photographic Evidence 122
Chapter 13 – The Texas Hair Samples 138
Chapter 14 – The Experts Weigh in 149
Chapter 15 – What to Make of it All 166
Acknowledgements 179
Sightings Appendix 180
References and Citations 201
Index 214
About the Author 222

Foreword

AS A SCIENTIFIC DISCIPLINE, cryptozoology (most simply defined as the study of variably large "hidden" animals not accepted by science) is considered typically to be the unwanted cousin of academic zoology. But as Bernard Heuvelmans and others have documented, many great zoological discoveries had cryptozoological roots in which the tales of native peoples and reports by travelers to other lands were a pathway to official discovery by researchers who put in the effort to explore these reports and ultimately obtain definitive evidence. Even today, there are cryptids yet to be admitted into the pantheon of zoological respectability, ranging from the fascinatingly likely to the fantastically unlikely.

In *Shadow Cats*, author Michael Mayes tackles a fascinating cryptozoological mystery that straddles two of the seven categories of cryptozoology as defined by Richard Greenwell in the Winter 1982 issue of the journal Cryptozoology: Category I (individual representatives of known, extant species whose…coloration or pattern is in some way extraordinary) and Category II (extant species unrecognized as existing in certain geographical areas). Large black cats fit the bill on both counts as the debate rages over the interpretation of such sightings and associated evidence.

Tangled up with this cryptozoological mystery are more mainstream zoological topics, namely the uncertainty about the current range and status of large cats formerly widespread in the U.S. and the uncertainty about the occurrence and frequency of melanism (resulting in an all black-haired animal) within those same species. For these compelling reasons, this book will be of interest to academic zoologists as well as their cousins in cryptozoology.

Mayes brings a refreshingly scientific and analytical perspective to the gathering of extensive data and the assessment of large black cat sightings and intriguing associated evidence. This requires deft maneuvering between the twin traps of denialism (practiced by too many scientists towards cryptozoology) and uncritical acceptance (practiced by too many acolytes of cryptozoology). Mayes strikes just the right balance between these two approaches.

No book-length treatments of this cryptozoological mystery exist, and previous articles just treat fragments of this mystery without exploring the full context necessary. Therefore, this is a most welcome addition to the literature of both crypto- and traditional zoology. While Mayes's geographic focus is primarily the southern U.S., this book will provide guidance to, and set a standard for, researchers investigating the large black cats reported both prowling, and teasing our imagination, in other parts of the world.

Angelo Capparella, Ph.D.
Associate Professor of Vertebrate Zoology
Illinois State University

The author on the hunt in the prime cougar habitat of central New Mexico. (Joey Breard)

Author's Note

> Beware of the night, child.
> All cats are black in the dark.
> — Jean Genet

CHASING A MYTH is difficult business. People are hesitant to talk about such things. They have many good reasons not to talk, especially to someone like me who is, essentially, a stranger. In many ways, we all remain stuck in junior high. We do not like being focused upon or scrutinized too closely. We do not want to be ridiculed or teased. Oh, we may say we do not care what others think, but precious few of us really mean it. I have stacks of interviews, emails, and other correspondence from people who contacted me with details about their own encounters with one of these shadow cats but who are adamant that they do not want any of it published. While I understand, at least to a degree, why someone would want to keep his/her experience private, I do feel it is slowing the process of solving this mystery. I hope the fact that this book treats the subject of black panther sightings seriously helps alleviate some of the fear of coming forward so many seem to feel.

When people do not want their stories published, you must seek information elsewhere, and I have attempted to do just that by way of the inaccurately named Freedom of Information Act. I wanted to find out what, if anything, our government knows about these mystery cats. First, contrary to what the name implies, the information is anything but free; you pay for it (boy, do you pay for it). Second, the government officials I dealt with, while cordial, were not helpful in the least. I was told time and again that my request for information was "too vague," and unless I had names, exact dates, and exact locations, they could not take the time to search. I bit my tongue when tempted to say, "If I had all that, I would not need you." Would you be surprised to find out that the Texas Parks and Wildlife Department is unable to do a search based only on a species of animal? It certainly surprised me. I mean, "wildlife" is part of their name, after all. The bottom line is that I would receive no helpful information from any government agency. I was on my own.

Writing this book has been both a joyful and miserable experience. I have been taken aback by just how long the entire process has taken. Talking to witnesses, placing and maintaining game cameras, conducting phone interviews, and the actual writing process takes an enormous amount of time. Mix in the fact that I am holding down a full-time job and have a family and all the responsibilities that come along with it, and it explains why this book took so long to complete. I cannot tell you how many times I thought about junking the whole thing. It was just so hard to find the time to do things the right way. It seemed I really was chasing shadows (hence, the title of the book) and would never finish. Now that it is over, I am glad that I did put my head down and fight through the self-doubt in order to complete the project.

While I hope the book is well-received, I find myself not worrying too much about that. I certainly did not start the project based on such a hope; rather, I felt that I had information that needed to be shared and disseminated. I almost felt a sense of duty to do so. Mostly, though, I felt a responsibility to the many witnesses who have trusted me with their experiences to complete the book. Their encounters deserved to be documented and preserved in a dignified way. I hope they know I did my best to do so.

I do not claim to be an expert on the subject of black panthers but do feel I have gained some insights into the phenomenon during my research that give me something unique to offer. I have done my best to present the material here in a level-headed and scientific manner, as well as posit some theories as to the possible identity of these mystery cats. My hope is that someone smarter than I will have his/her interest piqued and pick up the ball on this topic. Maybe then, we can get to the bottom of things.

If not, these creatures will remain little more than myths and legends; shadow cats.

Michael Mayes
Temple, Texas
July 2017

Preface

THIRTEEN-YEAR-OLD CHARLES ADAMS was in a rush. Good daylight had been burned while he sat in school until 3:00, and still more time was lost after he was released as he had to complete his daily chores. As was usually the case when he wanted to get in an afternoon hunt, things had taken longer than he would have liked and the sun was already low in the sky by the time he was able to finish up, grab his rifle, and head out for the woods. Charles figured he had at least an hour of good daylight left in which to hunt. It was not a lot, but it was better than nothing and he meant to make the most of it.

Since he did not have time to wander too far, Charles settled on hunting Hackberry Creek. It was nearby and wildlife used the creek bed as a thoroughfare. If he could get there by dusk, chances were good he would get a shot at something.

Upon arriving at the creek, Charles began quietly descending the slope toward a concealed spot near the bottom. A subtle noise stopped him in his tracks. He cut his eyes toward the area — no more than 25 feet away — from whence the sound had come, and listened. Something was definitely making its way toward the creek from the opposite bank. Charles flicked the safety off his .22 rifle, seated the stock against his shoulder, and waited.

Long seconds ticked by before a large black cat stepped out of the brush line and made its way to the bottom of the dry creek bed. Charles involuntarily lowered his rifle a bit to study the creature; when he did so, the cougar — even though it was black, that had to be what it was — turned and locked eyes with him. Charles watched in fear as the big cat gathered itself and tensed for a leap in his direction. Terrified, Charles raised the barrel of his .22 back into position. *Please let it be enough gun,* he prayed, and squeezed the trigger...

This book details the actual accounts of real people, including that of Charles Adams detailed here, based on personal interviews, newspaper archives, and other documented sources. The sheer number of black panther reports from across the United States precluded me from investigating them all; that being the case, I have primarily focused on accounts that have taken place in my home state of Texas and the region commonly referred to as the American South, though, outliers from as far west as California, as far north as Ontario, and as far east as North Carolina are included as well. The sightings I have chosen to chart and discuss in this book were those I deemed to be the most credible. Many sighting reports not discussed in detail in the main body of the book can be found in the Sightings Appendix. Additional information can be found at the *Texas Cryptid Hunter* website.

Introduction

BLACK PANTHER! The term conjures up all sorts of images in the mind's eye ranging from political activists to super heroes. In East Texas, where I grew up, when we heard the term black panther we immediately knew the speaker was talking about a large predator: a screaming, hissing, and bad-tempered cat roughly the size of a Great Dane. The womanish caterwauls and howls of these cats had chilled the blood of early settlers who had hacked an existence out of the piney woods and bottomlands of the region since at least the 1800s. To some, the black panther was a bad omen; a sign something terrible was about to happen. Other less superstitious types thought of them as nothing more than a predator: a reason to keep a close eye on their children and livestock. One thing all types of people living in East Texas and across the American South would have agreed upon is that the cats existed. They were as real as the more common bobcat, black bear, or coyote. This belief still holds sway among those whose families have inhabited the region for generations. Despite never having seen one of these shadow cats myself, I never doubted they were real until well into my adult years when I learned that mainstream science did not accept the existence of large, black, long-tailed cats. It was very clear that, according to wildlife experts, there was no such thing as a black panther.

I was quite surprised by this revelation. How could such a story have survived for 100-150 years without some basis in fact? I knew that many in my own family believed these cats existed, and stories of run-ins with them still circulated. I found it difficult to believe that a tall tale – a nice way of saying a fabrication – could resonate so strongly with so many people for so many years unless there was something tangible behind it.

It was at this point I discovered the black panther was thought of as a "cryptid." The term cryptid, can be loosely defined as an animal that may or may not actually exist: a creature not documented by science. Classic examples of cryptids would be the sasquatch, yeti, and Loch Ness monster. Some stretch the meaning of the term a bit farther and use it to describe so-called "Lazarus" species: animals thought to have been long extinct that may still exist in extremely remote locales. From time to time, this exact scenario has played out; for example, the rediscovered coelacanth falls into this category.

I became very interested in cryptozoology and began doing some research of my own. I found the whole topic fascinating; however, it did not take long before I realized that those interested in such things were considered, at best, fringe scientists and, at worst, outright kooks. Initially, I was offended by this reality. After all, I was no kook; at least I did not feel like one. Once I began researching various topics, however, I came to understand why so many felt this way about cryptids and those interested in them. For whatever reason, the subject seemed to be a magnet for all manner of, shall we say, eccentric types. I did not understand why this was the case, but it was undeniable. Looking around the internet for information on cryptids was a jarring experience. While there were a few sites and individuals out there who were truly attempting to get to the bottom of these mysteries in a scientific manner, they were few and far between. The field had truly been hijacked by the lunatic fringe. It was as if the doors to an insane asylum had been opened and every escapee handed a keyboard and his/her own website address on his/her way out.

After seeing the sheer amount of silliness out there in cyberspace, I decided to attempt to add a voice of sanity to the mix and, in 2008, started writing the *Texas Cryptid Hunter* website. I wanted to prove that one could be interested in topics that were somewhat unusual and not be a crazy person. While not a scientist, I wanted to examine these topics with a scientific eye. The blog has been, in my opinion, an overwhelming success with more than 1.5 million page views since its inception. There really was, it seemed, a thirst among the general public for a more levelheaded look at the cryptid phenomenon.

By far the most popular topic I have written about at the *Texas Cryptid Hunter* is the black panther. No other topic is even close. To say I was surprised by this would be an understatement. As I mentioned previously, where I grew up black panthers were nothing to get overly excited about. Certainly, they were not seen every day, but they were spotted often enough that they were not considered unusual. Many people, not unlike me not so long before, simply had no idea that these enigmatic cats were not supposed to exist. The people who had seen these animals had found out the hard way what I already knew: mainly, that if you reported seeing a black panther to wildlife officials, you would be treated as if you were reporting a unicorn sighting.

Still, the reports came flooding in to me at the site. Normal people, who did not sound crazy in the least, sharing a brief glimpse of something strange, unusual, and, sometimes, frightening. I published many of their encounter reports on the site, and each time I did it would generate a new wave of reports that flooded my inbox. Something was going on here. Were all of these people crazy, liars, or hoaxers? That seemed unlikely to me. Folks in Texas and the Deep South were seeing something… something matching the traditional description of a black panther. If these cats did not exist, what were they seeing?

Here was a mystery right in my own backyard! I resolved to Make every effort to get to the bottom of the black panther mystery. I began collecting reports, anecdotes, and even a handful of photos sent in by witnesses, and that has led me here to this book. While I had opinions on what might be behind the black panther phenomenon going into this project, I wanted to examine the evidence and follow it where ever it might lead. That is exactly what I have strived to do with this book.

I invite you to join me now; let us see where the evidence leads us.

1
A Matter of Semantics

So as not to be dismissed out of hand, let it be stated for the record that, according to mainstream science, there is no such animal as a black panther. The known big cats that have been given this moniker are either African or Asiatic leopards or New World jaguars exhibiting melanism. While American wildlife officials will express interest in sightings of cougars, ocelots, or jaguars, they more often than not will be uninterested and dismissive toward anyone who uses the term black panther. In their eyes, the use of this term proves the individual in question knows nothing about big cats and has no idea what he/she is talking about. Sighting reports of large black panthers are dismissed because no such animal exists.

Having said that, the fact that the black panther is not recognized by wildlife officials and biologists as a real flesh and blood creature has done little to sway the opinion of many rural residents of Texas and the American South who believe that these shadow cats are, indeed, real. At this point, the reader needs to understand that when the term black panther is used, witnesses are using a colloquialism: a catchall phrase, if you will, that is commonly used by laymen in the region to describe any large, black or very dark, long-tailed cat. Most of them do not know there is not supposed to be any such animal and are only describing what they have encountered in terms with which they are familiar. For their accounts to be dismissed out of hand solely because the term black panther is used in their descriptions is elitism at its worst.

Before delving further into this phenomenon, it is imperative to clear up some other terms and their definitions as well. The meaning of words often varies from region to region, and the term panther is no exception. To many, especially those who do not live in the South, a panther is the equivalent of a cougar, puma, mountain lion, or catamount (*Puma concolor*). These are all terms for the same animal. This is not the case in Texas or most of the southern United States. In these areas, when someone uses the term panther they are almost always describing a large, black, long-tailed cat. Here, the typical honey, gold, or tawny-colored puma is almost universally called a cougar or mountain lion. The only region of the South where this is not always the case is Florida, where the endangered Florida panther (*Puma concolor coryi*), a sub-species of puma, once roamed in great numbers and now struggles to survive in the Everglades. The plight of the Florida panther has been well publicized in the state, leading many citizens to understand that a panther and a puma are the same animal. This message was driven home in 1992 when the Florida Panthers hockey team of the NHL came to Miami. The team adopted the name of the endangered panther and created a logo featuring a golden-colored cat.

Florida remains the exception to the rule, however, as most people in the South picture a fierce black cat when they think of a panther. The prevalence of the panther as a high school mascot in Texas and other southern schools serves to underscore how deeply ingrained the mythos of this enigmatic cat is in the region. It also illustrates how southerners differentiate the appearance of a cougar from that of a panther. Many schools use the cougar as a mascot here in Texas, and they are represented by a typical tawny-colored cat, the mountain lion with which everyone is familiar or, in some cases, a cat in the dominant school color. Find a school using a panther as its mascot, however, and you will see it represented in quite a different manner. The panther will always be black. This trend can even be seen in the professional ranks, as the mascot for the Carolina Panthers of the NFL is a fierce black cat. This imagery resonates because it comes from a deeply embedded and long held belief that large, black cats, albeit in small numbers, do inhabit the wilder areas of our continent.

The difference between how a southerner differentiates a panther from mountain lion is important to know as many historical accounts use only the word panther when describing the animal in question. Often, somewhere else within the account, a description noting the animal was black will follow, but not always. My research has shown newspaper accounts from the days of early Texas typically used the terms catamount, puma, or lion when describing the more familiar cougar. For example, an article published in the *Dallas Morning News* on July 11, 1880, details the killing of a two-year-old child by a large cat. Note the terminology used to describe the cat in this article: "A puma which has been infesting the neighborhood of Pilot Grove for several weeks, yesterday tore to pieces and devoured the two-year-old child of a farmer living on the Burns tract."[1]

Another article, this one from the *San Antonio Daily Light*, was published on January 8, 1900, and describes an attack by an unknown assailant on a cow owned by a local. While the identity of the predator was not known, the assumption was that a big cat of some kind was the culprit. Note how the article outlines several possible suspects: "Some ferocious wild beast, believed to be either a wildcat, panther or Mexican lion attacked a cow belonging to a man named Wander, on Leal Street yesterday morning at 1 o'clock and bit the animal several times in the neck."[2]

Three different terms, describing three different species of cat, are used in the article. The term wildcat was most often used to describe a bobcat around the turn of the century; the term panther, as has been pointed out, described a large, black, long-tailed cat; and the term Mexican lion or Mexican tiger was used in the late 1800s and early 1900s to describe a spotted jaguar.

The colloquial differences between wildcats, panthers, and mountain lions in the South is further solidified by the way the United States Army uses the terms. It is common for military units to adopt a mascot or nickname. These mascots are often immortalized on the patches of the unit. Take, for example, the 81st Infantry Division – now the 81st Regional Support Command - that has adopted Wildcat as a nickname.[3] The patch for the 81st features a black but clearly short-tailed cat. It is obvious the cat that has been adopted is a bobcat. The 81st is using the term in the exact same manner as reporters from the late 1800s up through the early 1900s would have. The 66th Infantry Division has adopted the black panther as its mascot.[4] There are two iterations of this patch. One version shows the head of a ferocious and snarling black panther, but the body is not visible. In the alternate patch, the entire body of the cat is visible, long tail and all, as it leaps over a lightning bolt. These two distinguished military units have perfectly illustrated the difference between a wildcat and a panther as understood by most people in the American South.

It is very important to keep all of this in mind when reading historical accounts so as to get the clearest picture possible of what was going on at the time. Journalists were well aware of what terms they were using and what they meant. By differentiating between wildcats, pumas, Mexican lions, and panthers, reporters of the day were clearly drawing distinctions between those species. Many of these distinctions remain alive and well today.

There may be a biological entity responsible for the black panther sightings in Texas, or there may not, but conclusions should be drawn from the sighting reports, historical accounts, biological facts, and current scientific theories presented in this book and not solely on the use

The patch of the 81st Infantry Division (Wildcats) on the left as compared to one of the patches worn by the 66th Infantry Division (Black Panthers) on the right. (Priorservice.com)

of a term commonly used in the real world that is deemed inaccurate by experts. In addition, it is important to understand colloquial terms and language used during the mid to late 1800s and into the early 1900s if an accurate assessment on the possible existence of these cryptid cats is to be made, as failing to do so would be disingenuous and unscientific. So, too, would dismissing witness reports because said witness used a scientifically inaccurate term to describe what he/she saw. Throwing the baby out with the bath water due to semantics, as has so often occurred, is irresponsible and lazy.

2

Historical Accounts and Folklore

TALES OF BLACK PANTHERS PROWLING the countryside, swamps, bayous, and woods of Texas and the entire southeastern region of the United States are certainly nothing new. The legend has been around since the earliest settlers hacked an existence out of the North American wilderness and has become deeply ingrained in Texas and Southern culture. People who would take a long, sideways look at someone claiming to have seen bigfoot or a chupacabras would likely think nothing strange at all about a person claiming to have seen a black panther. To the people living in the more isolated and rural parts of the region, these cats are not considered anything unusual.

A conversation I had with a couple living outside of Dawson, Texas, several years ago highlights this point. One of their dogs had recently gone missing for several days, and they feared that a cat had taken him. "We have a couple of long-tailed cats come through here about twice a year," the husband said. "One tawny-colored one and one black. I hope one of them didn't get him."[5] When questioned further, he said he had seen both cats a handful of times over the last four or five years, but they had never bothered him or any of his animals before. It was exactly the kind of matter-of-fact comment that you often hear from rural Texans about these animals. For these folks, the panthers have always been here.

It is impossible to say for sure exactly how far back stories of large black cats go in Texas. Native American tribes who called Texas home passed down their history and stories orally and, almost without exception, did not write anything down. It is undeniable that cougars and panthers played significant roles in their mythology and religious beliefs;

exactly what role varied from tribe to tribe. For some, seeing a panther or hearing its scream was an evil omen, and some even associated these cats with witchcraft. Other tribes, notably in the southeast region of what is now the United States, interpreted things differently.

The ornate headdress (left) was worn by jaguar warriors into battle. The stone carving of a jaguar (right) adorns an Aztec pyramid in Teotihuacan. (Dmitri Rukhlenko and Del7891\Dreamstime.com)

In the American southeast, panthers were thought of as noble animals and powerful hunting medicine.[6] What is not as clear, due to differences in language and dialect, is whether or not these tribes differentiated between the more common tawny-colored cougar and black specimens. The waters become even more clouded when native peoples from Mexico and Central America are included in the mix. These tribes were as familiar with pumas as tribes to the north but were also well acquainted with the jaguar, which is known to exhibit melanism. The Aztecs felt the jaguar represented the god Tezcatlipoca, the deity of the night sky, and thought so much of the predator that they called the best soldiers in their army jaguar warriors. These warriors wore jaguar skins and headdresses into battle hoping the fighting spirit of these big cats would manifest in them and lead them to victory.[7] Most art left behind by the Aztecs portrays jaguars with the more common coat, which features prominent spots called rosettes. Some art, stone carvings in particular, depict jaguars without rosettes. What is not clear is whether or not this was done in an effort to depict a jaguar without spots, possibly a fully melanistic specimen.

Closer to home, the Alabama and Coushatta Indians have lived in the Big Thicket region of Southeast Texas since the 1780s, forced west of their original homelands by encroaching Anglo settlers. Howard Martin documented many folktales of the Alabama-Coushatta that were passed down orally from generation to generation. One such tale, detailed in his book *Myths & Folktales of the Alabama-Coushatta Indians of Texas*, features a black panther. In the tale, a large black panther saves a tribesman from the jaws of a monstrous lizard – something that is interesting in and of itself – and asks only that his "nephews" the wildcat and the domestic cat never be harmed in return.[8] The tale is interesting in that the black panther is portrayed as a patriarch of sorts to other, perhaps lesser, species.

Some ignore folklore of this nature due to the fact that humans in the tales communicate verbally with animals. This is common, especially in creation tales, among the myths of many if not most of the Native American tribes. Other legends from across the continent feature Indians conversing with everything from beavers to eagles. In almost all cases, the animals at the center of the folktale are real. Perhaps this particular tale from the Alabama-Coushatta is anecdotal evidence that the black panther is, or was, real as well.

Things become clearer once Anglo and Mexican settlers began making their way to Texas in the 1800s. The *Houston Morning Star* of November 19, 1844, reported the story of a woman in Nacogdoches County successfully fighting off a big panther that seemed intent on making her its dinner.[9] The *Houston Telegraph and Texas Register* of August 20, 1845, reported, "A 450-pound panther was killed by Mr. Whitehurst of Brazoria County."[10] It is almost a certainty that the weight estimate is greatly over-exaggerated here, but the story of an extremely large black panther being taken seems sound enough.

Noted Texas historian W.T. Block documented one particularly frightening encounter that occurred on September 17, 1881, involving two loggers. Henry Winters and Alfred Creswell were walking along a railroad track near present day Lumberton when they were attacked by two large black panthers. The two reported that they stood back-to-back for thirty to forty-five minutes attempting to beat off the attacking predators with only a couple of large sticks. The panthers eventually retreated into the thicket but not before ripping the trousers of the pair to shreds and inflicting some nasty gashes on the lower extremities of the two loggers.[11]

The reports were not limited to Texas, however, as on October 10, 1872, the *Galveston Tri-Weekly* reported the story of a Florida woman who had been killed and devoured by a large panther.[12] It is possible this report details the actions of a Florida panther and not a black panther. As discussed earlier, this is the one area of the southeastern U.S. where the term panther is often used to describe a tawny-colored cougar; however, this incident did take place in 1872, a time well before the plight of the Florida panther came to the fore. That being the case, it may very well have been a black cat that attacked the woman in question. In the June 1, 1874, edition of the *Galveston Weekly News*, the terrible fate of a Louisiana mule skinner was detailed. The article reads in part: "A colored man started to drive a team with provisions from his home near Delta to the interior of the parish. He had been gone about 15 minutes when the team came dashing back without the driver." Several men set out to see what was the matter and about a mile down the road encountered a terrible sight. "The body of the man was lying in the road, and a huge panther was standing over it, eating one of his shoulders."[13] The men fired on the panther but either missed it or failed to wound it mortally and it escaped into the woods.

One incident that became very well known in southeast Texas was the account of a riverboat captain named J.J. Jordan. The incident is documented in the January 14, 1897, edition of the *Galveston Daily News*. Captain Jordan was taking a load of supplies up the Sabine River to Brice's Landing (a log skidway) on his steamer, the *Robert E. Lee*. After making his delivery, Captain Jordan ran into low water and had to anchor up and await the incoming tide. At some point while anchored, the Captain's dogs started baying. Upon investigation, a large cat was seen onshore up a large cypress tree. The 14-year-old son of the Captain, one Robert Jordan, fired a shot that knocked what turned out to be a black panther from the tree. The dogs were off the boat and on the big cat almost instantly. The panther was quickly dispatched by the young Jordan, who skinned it and allegedly had it mounted as a trophy on the wall of the pilot house that housed his father's steamer.[14]

Another famous story of pioneer Texans encountering a ferocious black panther was a tale told by Southeast Texas and Big Thicket legend I.C. Eason. Eason grew up in the bottomlands of the Neches River and became most well-known for fighting the oil and timber companies that wanted to take his family's land. The land was never legally purchased or deeded but was settled by Eason's ancestors shortly after the Civil War. Eason was many things to many different people. He was a poacher to the Texas Parks and Wildlife Department, an outlaw in the eyes of the oil and timber companies, a hero to the Dog People of the contested river bottoms, and a genuine character to his friend Blair Pittman, who chronicled many of his tales in the book, *The Stories of I.C. Eason, King of the Dog People*. One thing nobody doubts is that Eason and his kin knew every critter that lived in the bottoms.

One story that Eason shared with Pittman was the story of how his grandmother, Becky Ard, took on a black panther — and won — years before. It seems some of the men were out cutting red oaks to make boards one day. One of the men's wives decided to bring them some dinner. Alone, she set out to make her delivery. She had almost reached her destination when she was attacked and killed. The men heard her scream and tore off to try and save her but found her mutilated body just 200 yards from safety. "A panther had got'er," Eason said. "Killed 'er and then ate both 'er breasts off. You see, she had been nursin' a baby. A panther will go for the breasts for the milk." Not long after, back at the Ard cabin, Eason's grandmother awaited the return of her husband. About the time she expected him to be home, she heard a scratching sound. At first, Mrs. Ard thought that her husband was trying to scare her. She quickly realized that was not the case when a black paw reached under the door. "She come down with that axe and chopped it off. She heard a scream that could've been heard for miles. Then it was gone," said Eason. Shortly thereafter, Mr. Ard returned, gathered his dogs, and the two of them went after the killer cat. With the help of the dogs, the pair successfully treed and dispatched the black panther. "To this day, I'm not real sure which one of 'em shot the panther," Eason related, "but Gran'ma? She nailed that panther's paw above her pieux door for good luck."[15]

Some have dismissed Eason's tale due to his comment about the panther being particularly interested in eating the breasts of this unfortunate lactating woman; however, this may not be wise as this very phenomenon has been mentioned by other prominent Texas folklorists. One such example comes from none of other than J. Frank Dobie, one of the most prolific authors and preservationists of Texas folklore in the history of the Lone Star State. In "The Panther's Scream," Dobie writes of the opinion of early Texas settlers that mothers' milk did, indeed, attract panthers. "What really made a panther hungry was the smell of a baby. Some people claimed a panther could locate a baby by scenting milk from its mother's breasts."[16] Whether the scent of her baby or the smell of mothers' milk that, no doubt, clung to her was the cause of this poor woman's demise will never be known, but the opinion of I.C. Eason that "a panther will go for the breasts for the milk" is not as outlandish a claim as it might, at first, seem and is not, on its own, a valid reason to doubt the story.

The tale told by one Emily Stacy of Montgomery County, Arkansas, back in the mid 1800s closely resembles the experience of Becky Ard shared by Eason. It seems Mrs. Stacy was home alone taking care of her children when a panther attempted to enter the family cabin. The creature persisted in its efforts to the point that Mrs. Stacy was afraid it might succeed in getting through the cabin door. Fearing for the safety of her family, she loaded a musket and fired through the wooden door in the hopes of frightening the big cat away. The strategy seemed to have been successful as the noisy efforts of the panther to get through the door ceased. The family stayed holed up in the cabin the rest of the night. It was not until the next morning that Mrs. Stacy dared open the door of the home and cautiously stepped out. She quickly discovered that her shot had done more than just scare the panther away, it had mortally wounded it. Lying dead on the porch at her feet was what she described as a black mountain lion.[17]

The Emily Stacy story is not the only historical connection between the state of Arkansas and the large black cats said to haunt the woods there. Arkansas-born artist Carroll Cloar (1913-1993) produced a beautiful painting titled *Story Told by My Mother* in which a woman is seen beating a hasty retreat from a very large black panther-like cat that has emerged from the nearby woods. The painting, currently on display at the Memphis Brooks Museum of Art in Tennessee, was, according to Cloar, inspired by tales of black panthers told to him by his mother when he was a youth.[18] Another accomplished Arkansan artist, William Rebsamen, produced a painting called *American Panther* featuring a large black cat cornered by dogs, making it clear black panthers are firmly ingrained in the lore of Arkansas.

The painting American Panther *by William Rebsamen is based on eye-witness accounts related to him by his fellow Arkansans.*
(William Rebsamen)

The accounts presented here do not prove the existence of a large, black, predatory cat in Texas or the American South. What they do prove is that the black panther phenomenon is not new and has been around since at least the 1800s.

Some skeptics might entertain the thought that there might have been a big black cat of some kind in Texas and the American South at one time, but no longer. If they ever existed at all, they must all be gone now: extinct. After all, no one is reporting sightings of black panthers anymore.

That could not be further from the truth.

3

Contemporary Black Panther Accounts

WHAT DISTINGUISHES A MYTHICAL BEAST from a documented animal? Most people's answer would include something along the lines of definitive evidence. In the case of the black panthers of Texas and the American South, the list of what might constitute definitive evidence could include convincing photographic or video images, or DNA left behind in spoor, such as scat or hair. Others take a harder stance and say that science demands a body; nothing less will suffice. Normal folks, though, generally do not engage in such discussions. They are just too busy going about the business of making a living. What is real to them is not based on what some scientist in a white lab coat tells them exists; rather, it is based on their own personal experiences. What they have heard with their own ears and what they have seen with their own eyes, that is what is real to them.

The black panther is as real to the people who inhabit the river bottoms, swamps, marshes, bayous and deep woods of the South as any other animal. It is no different than the coyote, alligator, fox, hog, or raccoon; it's just another member of the local fauna. Many of the people living in these regions do not even realize that science does not recognize the existence of these big cats and are stunned when informed of it. Some people become visibly upset and angry. They take the disbelief of mainstream scientists as a personal affront to their honor and integrity. More times than I can count over the years, I've heard people say, "I know what I saw and nobody can tell me any different," or "If those scientists would get out of their offices and spend a week in these woods, they'd change their minds pretty quick," or "I don't care what they say, those cats are real."

Whether people who claim to have seen these anomalous cats know it or not, there is precedent for mythical beasts springing from legend and lore and into the science books. The list of known animals once thought to be mythical, while not long, is impressive. The okapi, Komodo dragon, duck-billed platypus, mountain gorilla, and giant squid are just a few of the real-life creatures that were once treated as old wives' tales by academia. These animals had been described for years by indigenous peoples, but the stories were thought to be too fantastic to be taken seriously until specimens were actually collected, proving the legends to be true. Yes, some might argue, but these animals were discovered a long time ago. Surely, there is nothing the size of a black panther left to discover, especially within the borders of the most modern country in the world. The old stories may be as recent as the early 1900s, but no one is seeing these cats today, right?

Wrong.

Black panther sightings continue to be reported on a regular basis. I have already mentioned numerous accounts documented in newspapers from the late 1800s through the early 1900s (Chapter 2), so I will use this chapter to highlight sightings of a much more recent variety.

Herman Colyer is an 88-year-old retiree living in Bruceville, Texas. Recently, he shared with me his recollections of multiple sightings of what he called "black panthers" back when he was working clearing pipeline right-of-ways through the Piney Woods of east Texas in 1964: "I was working with another guy clearing the right-of-way for a pipeline that was going to be laid through the woods not too far from Livingston [Texas]. One morning, a little after sun up, he was sitting up running the Caterpillar and, all of a sudden, stopped and said, 'Look, there, Herman, a panther and two babies.' I looked and, sure enough, there was a Momma panther and two cubs walking across the right-of-way. We saw them several more times that year."[19]

Mr. Colyer went on to say he got a good long look at the cats as they were in no particular hurry to cross the 100-foot wide right-of-way and were no more than 25-30 yards away when he observed them. He described the largest cat as approximately the same size as a German shepherd and the two cubs as about twice the size of a normal house cat. "They were little bitty things," he said. Mr. Colyer went on to add that the cats had long tails that "kind of swished back and forth behind them" and that they were solid black.

An article published in the *San Francisco Chronicle* on August 9, 2009, reported the sighting of a black mountain lion by ranch owner Lynn Reed. Reed, the article points out, is an avid hunter and wildlife expert who says he and his wife watched what appeared to be a black mountain lion for more than 10 minutes in the foothills near Dublin in Alameda County. Reed described the cat: "He was black as can be with a head the size of a cantaloupe. We watched it for 10 minutes. I said to my wife, 'Look how its tail goes back and curls up, look how its shoulders move.' It was 3 feet long, the tail 2½ feet, maybe 60, 75 pounds."[20]

The sighting became even more credible when a surveyor named Art Whitten reported seeing a large black cat, matching the description given by Reed, the very next day in the nearby San Ramon Hills. Here is Whitten's account, as reported in the article:

> I was setting up an aerial panel and I felt something watching me. I turned and he was sitting in a ravine, 100 feet away. Of course, at first I was nervous, but he showed no interest in me. I've seen a lot of mountain lions, and I'd estimate it as the average size of a mountain lion.[21]

During the encounter, Mr. Whitten phoned his supervisor, Barry Williams, twice to report on what he was seeing while in the field. When asked his opinion on Whitten's report, Mr. Williams said only, "He has seen lions before and I know he isn't off his rocker."

A native of North Carolina, Dr. Angelo Capparella, now an Associate Professor of Zoology and Curator of Vertebrates at Illinois State University, took an interest in the black panther phenomenon as a young man and investigated several reports. Dr. Capparella is a Fellow of the American Ornithological Union and Research Associate of the Field

Museum of Natural History. Known primarily for his work with birds, Dr. Capparella has been exploring uninhabited regions of South America to gather data on the effect of river barriers to avian evolutionary development since 1982. His work has been invaluable and, besides the data collected on the effect of river barriers on the avian evolutionary process, he has been directly involved in the discovery of three new species. Dr. Capparella has been gracious enough to dig back through his archives to provide several black panther sighting reports he collected back in the early 1970s.

Here is an excerpt from a letter dated February 15, 1972, that Dr. Capparella received from a Wildlife Patrolman T.H. Robbins:

> On or about February 5, 1972, in the Gull Rock section of Hyde County, a large brown cat with a long tail was sighted lying in a field but ran into the woods when the person observing him attempted to approach. The subject said the cat looked like a mountain lion. The subject is a hunter and his observation should be at least fairly accurate. I have always received reports on cats, such as a big black one and a mountain lion. I had a report on two last year in other areas of Hyde County. I cannot verify any of them...[22]

In August of 1972, Dr. Capparella and two associates traveled to the Mattamuskeet area to meet with Mr. Robbins and investigate the reports of panthers in the area. Robbins took the three investigators to areas from which he had received black panther sighting reports. Dr. Capparella realized that the anecdotal information he was receiving from Mr. Robbins would never serve as proof but did express his hope that the accounts would "...give an idea of the prevalence of people who believe they have seen a panther(s)."[23]

Mr. Robbins shared the details of numerous sightings with Dr. Capparella and his associates that day. Following are excerpts taken directly from Dr. Capparella's notes regarding a few of those reports:

> Two or three weeks ago, two men in a truck saw a black cat

with a long tail, as big as a dog, on Bull Hill Road. They saw it in the evening on the road in front of their truck.

Within the last month (September) another man saw, in the same area, a similar cat.

Another man told us that four or five years ago, on the road to Rose Bay, he had seen a black cat.

Last year, near Fairfield, a black cat was seen.

A couple of months ago, a man told Robbins that he had seen three black cats with long tails around some equipment where they were doing logging. The cats were about two feet high. This was on Seagoing Road in Tyrrell County.

A man saw a cat two-feet high, black with a long tail, between Bellhaven and Washington, where one turns off for Bath.

Perhaps, the most interesting report of all was related to Dr. Capparella by another local Wildlife Patrolman. Here is the account, as it appears in Dr. Capparella's notes: "Wildlife Patrolman C.I. Willis told us of a sighting he made about a year ago at a wooden bridge near Seagoing Road (Tyrrell County). He saw what appeared to be a mother panther and three kittens. All were black. He was about two hundred yards from them and observed them through binoculars. The time was mid-afternoon."[24]

This report is fascinating for two reasons. First, this sighting took place on the same road where another man had reported seeing three large black cats just weeks before. Second, in this case, the witness was a trained wildlife officer observing the cats through binoculars in the middle of the day. Misidentification seems highly unlikely in this scenario.

While the bulk of my research has been focused on Texas, it is clear that sightings of large, black, long-tailed cats are not confined to the Lone Star State. As the sighting of Lynn Reed, so well documented by the *San Francisco Chronicle*, and the spate of sightings in North Carolina, investigated by a young Dr. Angelo Capparella, prove, the black panther phenomenon is alive and well in these modern times with sightings reported from the Pacific to the Atlantic coasts. It is as if a sort of black panther Manifest Destiny has taken place.

While sightings have been reported from sea to shining sea, the bulk of these visual encounters have taken place in the southern half of the contiguous United States. Here in Texas, the black panther remains very much alive in the psyche of the state's residents, and sightings continue, unabated. I believe the following two accounts, which were featured by Ken Gerhard and Nick Redfern in their book *Monsters of Texas*, demonstrate this fact.

Ryan and Lisa Knott live in southeast Texas in Big Thicket country near Warren. They are journalists who publish a weekly newspaper dedicated to their corner of east Texas. The pair have claimed sightings of black panthers for years on their land and have seen the big cats roaming a dirt road near their home.[25]

In 2007, a flap of sightings took place in the northeastern part of Texas. Cherokee County residents called in multiple sightings of a large black panther to authorities. Some witnesses claim they spotted not only the full-grown panther but three cubs as well. About a week later, and less than 50 miles to the north, in Upshur County, locals near Raintree Lake began to lose pets and livestock to an unknown predator. They began to hear terrifying screams coming from the forest at night around the same time. One Mitchell Bransford claimed to have come face to face with what he described as a "big black panther." Mr. Bransford insisted he had a good, long look at the animal in question. "I'm not talking about a glance, I'm talking straight at him and him just looking at me."[26]

Travis Lawrence is a life-long hunter, outdoorsman, and resident of east Texas. He has taught in the public school system for years and is now planning on attending seminary in order to become a pastor. He is a man of impeccable character whom I am proud to have known and called a friend for over a decade. I had known Travis several years before he shared his own black panther sighting with me. This is his story, in his own words:

"When I was young man, my father leased a large cattle ranch for us to hunt and camp on. This was a 400-acre piece of pristine hardwood bottomlands filled with deer and hogs. It is located in Anderson County, Texas, along Ioni Creek a few miles north of Highway 294 between the towns of Slocum and Alto. It was about a 15-minute drive from the house we lived in. The following incident occurred during the rut of the fall deer season. I cannot recall the exact year, but I was approximately 12 years-old. November of 1998 would be a good guess.

I was hunting a box blind we called 'The Gate Stand' near the entrance gate of this property. I was using an outstanding hunting rifle that my dad had recently acquired. It is a Remington 700 Sendero model chambered in .270 Winchester that wore a 6-18x50mm Bushnell Scope. I still hunt with this rifle nearly two decades later, and I say this because the rifle and scope are important pieces to the story. My dad dropped me off to hunt this stand –probably after picking me up from school – while he went farther back on the property to hunt a different stand.

It was cool and overcast. I remember seeing a few does meandering through the goatweeds and other scrub brush near me. There was also a partially obscured hill about 400 yards away that I had seen a few deer cross over. Not having any binoculars with me, I would look at these deer in my 18x scope, twice the magnification of a typical deer rifle scope. I could see them very well even though they were so far outside of my shooting range. I then recall seeing a larger deer step out on that hill with a doe. Even at 400 yards, I could tell it was a buck with my naked eye. I immediately found it in my scope and beheld a marvelous specimen of mature east Texas buck. He was probably an 8 point with about a 17" inside spread. He was much too far away to shoot at, but I watched him appear several times on this hill as he chased a doe back and forth. This is commonly seen during rutting activity. The two animals then wandered off outside of my view. A short while later, I saw what I assumed was a different deer cross over this same hill. I thought it was a doe, but I looked through my scope at her anyway to confirm my suspicion. It was indeed a mature doe. Not seeing anything else, I sat back in my chair and continued to watch.

A few seconds later, I saw a pitch black figure appear out of the brush and walk along the same line the doe had just traveled. It was about the same size as the doe, which I would guess was about 120 lbs. My first thought was that this was a hog. But even at 400 yards with my naked eye, it looked a little different. It was almost a shiny black. Hogs have matted hair that's mixed with greys and browns and mud, giving their hide a dull look. This looked clean and sharp. I immediately raised my scope. What I saw in my scope perplexed me at first. The weeds and such were approximately two feet tall and obscured the lower portions of the animal. It was traveling in a vector almost directly away from me. It was moving slowly and methodically. I could not identify it, but I could tell it was not a hog just by the way it moved. Then it stopped. While it was stopped, I saw its tail swish up behind it out of the weeds. It was at this moment that I knew exactly what it was. There was no doubt in my mind that I was staring at a large black cat. Its tail had to be as long as the cat was. The way its tailed swished up reminded me of the housecats we had at home. I remembered watching them raise their tail and wiggle it a little before pouncing on some poor unsuspecting grasshopper. A few seconds later, the animal disappeared over the hill and was never seen again. There was no doubt in my mind that I had seen a large black cat stalking a deer. I saw it for approximately 10-15 seconds.

My dad was not surprised when I told him about it later that night after he picked me up and we headed back home. We had long heard stories of mountain lions and panthers. We had even heard the typical "woman screaming" sound that everyone in east Texas blames on the large cats. The fact that the feline I witnessed was pitch black was not significant to me until many years later when I became aware that such an animal in that color scheme had not been officially catalogued. That was almost 20 years ago, but its image has remained burned in my memory as if it happened yesterday.[27]

Travis Lawrence had an unusually lengthy sighting of a large black cat while hunting as a boy in Anderson County, Texas.
(Chris Buntenbah)

Travis Lawrence's sighting is unique in that he was able to watch the animal in question for 10-15 seconds, an unusually long time. This would make the possibility of a misidentification far less likely than it would be in a visual lasting only 2-3 seconds. Already an experienced hunter at age 12, Lawrence was familiar with the fauna native to the woods of east Texas. This was something different, and his story has not changed at all since I have known him. Too, the nonchalant attitude of his father after being told of the sighting is typical of most rural east

Texas residents. If they have not seen a big black cat or heard a panther screaming themselves, they almost always know someone who has. The other factor that makes this sighting account different is that I have a personal relationship with Travis. He is one of the two or three straightest arrows I have ever met. I have never heard him utter an untruth and would trust him with my life. I believe Travis Lawrence saw something for which he cannot account.

I have received many black panther sighting reports over the last few years. The reports that follow are just a sampling of what I have in my records and are typical of what I hear from witnesses claiming to have had a run-in with these anomalous big cats. While shorter than the accounts previously discussed in this chapter, they are, nonetheless, important anecdotal evidence illustrating the fact that people are seeing something to which they are attaching the moniker of black panther. The reports are unedited and exactly as I received them. For reasons of both the practical and legal kind, I have withheld the names of the individual witnesses.

> Yesterday morning I was sitting on my back porch drinking coffee and watching my deer feeder which is about 40-50 yards from my house. Time was 6:30 a.m. I picked up my binoculars to make sure they were sighted in when I saw a dark form move into the area right behind my deer feeder. My first thought was it was a deer. It was not a deer but a large dark colored cat. The cat walked across the opening and back into the woods. I would guess the cat to be 30-36 inches tall and weigh around 50 pounds with a tail that had to be 2-3 feet in length. We live back in the woods of east Texas between Hardin and Hull Texas. I watched the cat through my binoculars for 10-15 seconds. I don't care what the biologists say, I know what I saw. At work this morning a couple of other people have witnessed similar cats in the past.
>
> November 22, 2010
> Hull, TX

Last week while hunting in my deer stand in Llano, TX, I saw a large black cat. At first I thought it was a bobcat and rejected the fact that it may be a black cougar but as I looked at it harder I noticed the cat was abnormally large and had a tail as long as its body, and he was absolutely black. In a daze I grabbed my gun and shot twice at him but missed before he tauntingly turned around and walked off. I later found out my gun's scope had been knocked off sight. I told the land owner and he said he has seen him before. To me I have all the proof I need to know the cats are real.

November 9, 2011
Llano, TX

I thought I was crazy but glad there are more like me. I was walking my small dog in a small wooded area near Klein High School in Klein, TX. Down a small dirt road, I saw a large black cat. It stopped and faced me and just looked at us. It looked pretty large and, having raised domestic cats of all breeds, I know this was not a domestic. It was very intimidating. I walked behind a large fence and looked back and he was still in the same position. I tried to hurry back to get my phone and he was gone.

July 6, 2012
Klein, TX

My grandparents used to live outside of Salado, TX on a large ranch and had property that backed up to Stillhouse Hollow Lake. On several occasions while hunting with my father when I was younger we would see a very large solid black cat with a long tail across one of the coves near the bank. We also saw the prints on our side of the lake and numerous times my family members would hear the screams from some sort of cat. Not sure what it was but my Dad always said it was a panther!!

February 13, 2013
Salado, TX

Contemporary Black Panther Accounts   25

I saw a young, 4-foot-long, male black panther nailed to a fence post in Kaufman County back in 1984. I was 18 at the time and just assumed everyone knew these cats were in the Trinity River Valley. I sure wish I had taken pictures and knocked on that rancher's door to get the story.

December 10, 2013
Kaufman County, TX

My grandfather and I, on our family's ranch in Lingleville, TX (About 75 miles south west of Fort Worth), saw a black cat with a long tail while feeding cattle. My great grandfather always told stories of seeing one on occasion. I'm a believer. There's no doubt in my mind of what it was. They're around.

November 17, 2013
Lingleville, TX

I've seen a large black cat south of Sierra Blanca (next to Redlight Mill). It was too big to be a house cat and was larger than a bobcat. It had a long tail like that of a mountain lion.

May 5, 2014
Sierra Blanca, TX

I, too, have seen a black panther near Hooks and Red River Bottoms. Saw the panther trailing a deer with another witness. 1993.

September 17, 2014
Hooks, TX

I also saw a cat that matches your description. It was autumn of 2005, I was driving on CR 532 approx. 2-3 miles from Gonzales toward Moulton, it was after work so approx. 5:15 –5:30 pm, it crossed in front of me toward some old chicken houses on left. I was totally amazed he leapt from the side of road on right of me to middle of road and another jump he was on the side of the road so graceful and had a very large body it seemed to drop down from belly low toward ground. The size reminded me of adult German shepherd, but it in no way a dog. It was so beautiful. The cat also had a bit of black stripy [sic] like marks of side of body. It was so graceful and I told people and of course they did not believe. A year or so later I ran into the game warden that covers Gonzales area and told him about the cat. I don't know if it was his demeanor, but he seemed not to believe me.

November 24, 2015
Brazoria, TX

I moved out by Churchill bridge in Brazoria, by the San Bernard River, I was looking out my kitchen window and saw a black cat, I was thinking, "Wow, he is big," then it turned and started slowing walking and I saw how big, and a long tail, really cool looking too, He moved so slow like a wild cat would, I could not get my camera fast enough to snap a photo, Also saw a big bobcat on this property, My Dad working for the refuge here and said he has heard of the jaguar sighting.

January 6, 2016
Gonzales, TX

Hi. My name is [redacted] and I live outside of Paris, Texas. My husband pastors a small country church that is about 15 miles northeast of Paris. This happened 5-6 years ago. I believe it was late summer/early fall in the late afternoon. My daughter and I had been out riding horses and were in the car headed back home. This happened on CR 45600 just off of FM 1502 in far northeastern Lamar county (nearly to the Red River county line). I was driving slowly because we were looking at one of our church member's horses. When we came over the crest of a little hill there was a black panther sauntering across the road in front of us! Maybe 10-15 yards away. He never got in a hurry and acted like it never saw us. I was stopped and watching it and I remember thinking am I really seeing this? The mascot of the school district I work for is a panther and I kept thinking it looks just like the North Lamar panther! It was large and black, its feet were huge and its tail hung down in the back and curled (like a backward "J"). It walked across the road and into the pasture on the other side. A few days later we were having a fellowship at our church and another lady was telling the church member who had the horses that we were looking at that she was driving past on the same road and across from where his horses were, a black panther was just sitting there! I have watched for it ever since but never seen it again.

July 24, 2016
Paris, TX

The reports above certainly do not prove the existence of the mythical black panther. They do, however, prove that this is not strictly a legend that died out in the late 1800s or early 1900s. The stories have never gone away, and sightings have never stopped. I strongly suspect that many other sightings go unreported for a variety of reasons. In many cases, the witness does not feel he/she has seen anything unusual. As mentioned previously, people living in the more rural areas of Texas and the American South have grown up with the notion that a black panther is just another animal that lives in the woods. In other cases, witnesses are simply not sure to whom to report a sighting. Others, perhaps wiser (jaded?) to the attitude of the Texas Parks & Wildlife Department and other wildlife agencies towards the possible existence of these cats, know that their report will, in all likelihood, not be taken seriously.

Most of the reports I receive are very much like those listed. They are brief and innocuous, with the witness getting only a quick glimpse at an animal that hastily retreats into the woods, brush, or high grass; however, that is not always the case. Some reports come from people who claim they got a little too close to one of these cats and came away badly frightened and shaken by the experience. One such incident was related to me by Charles Adams of Hurst, Texas. Mr. Adams was kind enough to relate a frightening incident that he experienced back in 1964-1965 when he was about 13 years old and living in Hill County, Texas. This is his story, in his own words:

> I was about, oh, 13 and I was hunting after school just west of Hillsboro, Texas in the Hackberry Creek bed right behind the National Guard Armory off highway 22. It was about 5:00 p.m. and still fully daylight when right across the creek I saw the large black animal come out of the brush on the bank of the creek. I was startled and just stared at it. I wasn't sure if my .22 rifle would do anything other than piss it off. I was only, maybe, 25-feet from it, if that far. I could clearly identify it as a black cougar, panther, whatever you choose to call it. It growled and then turned toward me and crouched and I opened fire. I emptied my rifle into it. I could see the rounds striking it in the right shoulder area. It backed up, screaming, and I left the other way rather quickly myself. I went home to get a bigger gun and came back. I hunted but couldn't find anything.[28]

While the experience of Charles Adams must have been intense, an even more harrowing report came to me in January of 2014 from Amanda Ward:

> The facts are simple. On December 31, 2013, I went to give the horses extra alfalfa at about 10:00 p.m. as a 19-degree overnight temperature was expected. On cold nights, this was routine. I walked to the back gate, opened the horse trailer parked there to store hay, got out 3 flakes of alfalfa. Closed the trailer up... (All of which makes a fair amount of noise.) Then I began to call the horses by yelling all of their names at the top of my lungs. I stood in silence, listening for their approach and waiting. Nothing. So, I started yelling again. Then, off to my right, along the fence line in an area of serious overgrowth, I could hear some-

thing start running toward me. This was not a scampering sound. Something meant business.

There was no doubt in my mind that the charge toward me was intentional. Whatever was coming was fast and serious and certainly NOT horses. I was wearing my puffy winter coat with David's thick winter coat over it, a hat and the hood pulled up over it. My point is, I looked quite a bit larger than I actually am, a fact that may have saved my life that night. By the time the charger arrived in my sight, I already had retreated backwards several steps, stomping my feet and yelling, "You get out of here!!" I held my arms up and out to make myself look large. I got 1 glimpse of a large black cat. Not a domestic shorthair, I described it to my fiancé, "I'd tell you it was a mountain lion, but it was too dark." I did not mean dark outside, I meant the fur appeared black. The animal stopped its charge at a horse trough where it crouched on the side that was away from me. At this point, it was about 12-feet away.

I continued my backward stomping retreat with my arms in the air, yelling, "You get out of here!" all the way to my porch... approximately

Amanda Ward of Ellis County, Texas was charged by what she describes as a large black cat in October of 2013. Her horses have sustained injuries inflicted by an unknown predator multiple times since the first incident. (Gail Kennedy)

> 60 yards. I believe that the black panther (cat of some kind) was about 90 pounds. This is based on my Catahoula Leopard dog being 88 pounds... and the animal I saw was similar in size, but longer. Just a few days later, David saw it at our fence line. He ran in to get a rifle, but it was gone before his return. We have had several horse injuries that look like they came from attacks. The horses are the best indicator of when the cat is near, as they are not scared of coyotes or other familiar animals, but react with a serious fearful frenzy at times. I believe the cat to be close enough to pose a danger when the horses behave like that. I also want to note that I told this story to many people around here... they all have seen the black cats, or know someone else who has.[29]

This report was unusual in several different ways. First, the cat was seen at very close range. Second, the cat exhibited unusually aggressive behavior. Third, a second sighting by the original witness's fiancé quickly followed on the heels of the first incident. Finally, unusual behavior by, and injuries to, the horses on the property were reported. I quickly replied to Amanda and she graciously allowed me to visit the property and deploy multiple game cameras. The cameras – never fewer than two or more than four – stayed up on the property for the next two years. While a surprising variety of wildlife was documented over that time, no photos of a cat matching the description given by Amanda were obtained.

The lack of photographic evidence does not mean Amanda is not telling the truth about her experience. A well-known, and admittedly overused, axiom among those who investigate cryptozoological matters is that absence of evidence is not evidence of absence. Big cats are notoriously elusive and often have large home ranges. It is quite possible that whatever frightened Amanda that night is only in the general vicinity of her property for a few days each year. If so, patience is the key as even the best game camera can keep watch on only a couple of hundred square feet.

The reports detailed in this chapter range from California in the west, to North Carolina in the east, to Texas and the American South, and cover a period of several decades. They are but a few of the accounts I have received over the last several years. While anecdotal evidence of this nature does not prove black panthers exist, I feel strongly the reports absolutely confirm the black panther phenomenon that existed at least as far back as the early 1800s remains alive and well into the present day. It begs the question: What are people seeing?

4

Is There Enough Suitable Habitat?

THOSE WHO ARE SKEPTICAL that a large black cat could possibly exist in Texas, or anywhere else in the American South, argue that there is a lack of suitable habitat in the region. They say there simply is not enough wilderness, undeveloped property, forests, or bottomlands left in the continental United States to support such a creature. While development and logging have certainly taken their toll on the forests of the region, most people would be shocked at just how much forestland and wilderness remain. According to the National Forest Service, there are an estimated 307 million hectares of forestland in the United States. This equates to 34 percent of the total land area of the country. While this is down considerably from the estimated 423 hectares of forest land in what would become the United States in 1630, there remains a vast amount of heavily wooded, wild, and sparsely populated land in this country.[30]

Here is a breakdown of how much forest land remains in the thirteen states generally referred to collectively as the "American South." The states are presented alphabetically followed by the number of acres of forest in the state, the percentage of the state's land covered in forest, the number of National Forests in the state, and the number of State Forests present. National Preserves, National Grasslands, and Wilderness Areas are included in the acres of forest in a state but not necessarily counted as a National Forest due to their special designation. This could cause discrepancies with some sources as to how many National Forests are in a particular state. Likewise, it should be noted that arboreal areas, grasslands, and other special areas are included by some states under the State Forest umbrella and not by others. This could cause discrepancies with some sources as to how many State Forests are in a particular state.

State	Acres of forest	Pct.	N.F.	S.F.
Alabama	23.0 million[31]	69.9%	4	5
Arkansas	18.4 million[32]	55.0%	2	1
Florida	17.3 million[33]	50.0%	3	35
Georgia	24.8 million[34]	67.0%	2	3
Kentucky	12.4 million[35]	48.0%	1	7
Louisiana	14.0 million[36]	50.0%	1	1
Mississippi	19.8 million[37]	65.0%	6	0
N. Carolina	18.6 million[38]	60.0%	4	10
Oklahoma	12.0 million[39]	28.0%	1	0
S. Carolina	13.0 million[40]	67.0%	2	5
Texas	62.4 million[41]	38.0%	4	5
Tennessee	14.0 million[42]	52.0%	1	15
Virginia	15.7 million[43]	62.0%	2	24

In total, the region traditionally known as the American South holds 265.4 million acres of forest land. As of 2012, the United States had 766 million acres of forest land,[44] meaning that the American South contains 35 percent of all the forests in the country. If Alaska, which has an astounding 129.0 million acres of forested land,[45] is removed from the equation, the American South has 42 percent of the forestland in the contiguous 48 states. Although it is true that the forests of the southern United States are more fragmented than they used to be due to logging and development, there remains more than enough wild land to support a breeding population of big cats.

The mountain lion is beginning to creep back into areas from which the species was extirpated in the late 1800s–early 1900s. If the cougar can do so, it stands to reason that another cat of similar size and stature could do the same. Of course, some would argue that the return of the cougar to its old home range could be the reason for modern black panther sightings – a topic that will be discussed in Chapter 7 – but, either way, there would appear to be enough space for at least a small breeding population of big cats to thrive and, for the most part, remain out of sight.

Although there is a lot of forestland in the American South, that does not necessarily mean all the forests there are rich and healthy environments. Certainly, the practice of clear cutting native hardwoods and replanting fast growing slash pines affects the ecosystem of a region. While these replanted forests are not quite as sterile as many initially believed them to be, they are devoid of fruit-producing hardwoods and most types of underbrush, severely limiting their ability to sustain a population of most types of wildlife. Fortunately, there remain vast tracts of hardwoods in the region that produce prodigious amounts of acorns, hickory nuts, black walnuts, pecans, and the like. This food base supports large populations of white-tail deer, feral hogs, and other smaller mammals, all of which could serve as a solid prey base for a population of big cats.

Wildlife biologist Dr. John Bindernagel, who visited the Texas-Louisiana region in 2001 and 2002, was impressed with the richness and scope of the mixed deciduous forests found there in comparison to the conifer dominated forests of the Pacific Northwest. Dr. Bindernagel recognized and commented on the value and productivity of deciduous forests in terms of wildlife habitat and stated that any large species of mammal living in southern forests would almost certainly require a smaller home range than an animal of the same species living in a northern coniferous forest.[46] What this implies is that, despite some fragmentation, the woods of the American South are more than adequate in size, scope, and richness of resources to support a breeding population of large cats.

Narrowing our focus just a bit, there also remains plenty of suitable habitat in the Lone Star State in which a population of big cats could thrive. Texas, due mostly to its immense size, is surprisingly diverse geographically. It is much more than the dusty desert so often portrayed in western movies. Texas stretches across four major physical regions of

The mixed deciduous forests of the American South are incredibly rich and sustain numerous species that might serve as a prey base for a population of big cats. (Chris Buntenbah)

North America. The major geographical regions of Texas are the Mountains and Basins, the Great Plains, the Central Plains, and the Gulf Coast Plains.

The Mountains and Basins Region lies in far west Texas and is often called the Trans-Pecos. The Mountains and Basins Region is a subregion of the Rocky Mountains, which stretch from Canada to Mexico. It is a rugged, sparsely populated area filled with mountains, canyons, and dry highlands. This is the home of Big Bend National Park. It is also one of the few areas in Texas recognized by the Texas Parks and Wildlife Department as having a breeding population of mountain lions. Many suspect that if jaguars are crossing into Texas from Mexico, this is the area where it is most likely occurring.

The Great Plains is a vast area that stretches north to south from central Canada, through the heartland of the United States and Texas and into northern Mexico. For the most part, it consists of flat grasslands. This is one of the flattest areas on earth and was once home to millions of American bison (*Bison bison*). The Great Plains Region becomes more rugged as it stretches into central Texas and forms the famed Texas Hill Country, an area rich in sightings of large black cats. Rainfall typically averages 15-20 inches per year in the westernmost area of the Texas Great Plains and 20-30 inches per year farther east.

The area generally considered North Texas, which includes the major cities of Abilene, Wichita Falls, Denton, and Fort Worth, is actually the southernmost portion of the Central Plains Region of the United States. The geography is diverse and ranges from rolling hills and prairies in the westernmost part of the region to hardwood forests back to the east. Post and blackjack oaks, hickories, elms, cedar, mesquite, and pecan trees thrive here. It is true that much of the hardwood forests are now gone – cut down by farmers eager to farm the rich soil of the region – but lush greenbelts remain, especially along the rivers and creeks of the region, and still provide a healthy habitat for feral hogs, white-tail deer, and many smaller mammals. The area, especially the northernmost stretches, has been the point of origin for a multitude of black panther reports over the years.

The easternmost region of Texas is the Gulf Coastal Plains. This is the largest region in Texas and covers approximately 40 percent of the state's land area. The Gulf Coastal Plains contain some of the best habitat in the state for wildlife and is incredibly diverse. Piney woods, lush plains, and dense brush lands are all present. The soil is rich and vast tracts of land are lightly populated and reserved for farming and ranching. This region is home to four different National Forests; the Sam Houston National Forest, Angelina National Forest, Davy Crockett National Forest, and Sabine National Forest. Each of these forests is unique and provides large areas of heavily wooded, prey-rich environments suitable for a big cat.

The Gulf Coastal Plains is also home to the Big Thicket National Preserve. Set aside because of its interesting plant and animal life, the Thicket is a mix of upland pine forests, river and creek bottomlands, meadows, sandy hills, hardwood forests, swamps, and bayous; the Preserve is often referred to as the biological crossroads of North America. The Big Thicket National Preserve is an amazingly rich environment that could easily support a population of large predators. In fact, it once did just that as a large population of black bears (*Ursus americanus*) once made this area of east Texas home before being extirpated in the early 1900s by hunters. The Big Thicket is also a very unfriendly and harsh environment for humans, making it the ideal place for a furtive species to live in obscurity. This area of the Gulf Coastal Plains Region is historically rich in black panther reports, and sightings continue to pour in from the area even today.

Once one understands the geography of Texas, as well as the sheer scope of the state, it is plain to see there is enough lightly populated land and wilderness left here to support a population of big cats. As reports continued to roll in on a nearly weekly basis, I wondered if there was a way to zero in on just where it might be most fruitful to search for these shadow cats. In the hopes of better understanding the black panther phenomenon and narrow down the vast search area, I decided to begin charting the sightings that I deemed to be credible. The results can be viewed on an interactive distribution map that can be accessed via a link on the *Texas Cryptid Hunter* website (www.texascryptidhunter.blogspot.com). I have currently charted the location of 148 credible sightings. I have taken in at least twice that many reports, but these 148 are the accounts I feel are most likely genuine and not hoaxes or cases of mistaken identity.

My hope was that by keeping a careful record of where the most credible sightings took place, a pattern might emerge. I was not disappointed. As the sightings piled up, a definite pattern did begin to take shape. By a wide margin, the majority of black panther sightings have been reported in the eastern half of the state. This, in my opinion, is no accident.

The eastern portion of Texas receives far more rainfall than does the rest of the Lone Star State. The Gulf of Mexico reigns supreme as the chief weather-maker here and is responsible for nearly all the precipitation that falls in east Texas. Systems blowing in off the Gulf range in intensity from gentle showers up to major hurricanes. In addition, the warm, moist air from the coast rides dominant air currents into the central portion of the state where it often reacts with cooler, drier air spilling down from the Great Plains. The results can be quite spectacular in the form of serious, and sometimes tornadic, thunderstorms. The bottom line is simple: the areas closest to the Gulf of Mexico get the most precipitation, and it is from these areas that most of the black panther sightings in Texas originate.

When one compares the sightings distribution map with the average annual precipitation map this pattern is plain to see. The bulk of the sightings come from areas receiving 32-48+ inches of rain a year. Even the sightings that have come from the Texas Hill Country just west of San Antonio fall into this pattern. If the precipitation map is examined carefully, a distinct bow to the west in the dark green area that indicates annual precipitation of 32-48 inches is evident. This is the exact area where the majority of Hill Country sightings have occurred. The pattern is easily discernible and seems indicative of the behavior of a living species. It does not seem likely that people living in areas receiving 32 or more inches of rainfall per year are more prone to misidentify known wildlife, suffer hallucinations, or submit hoaxed reports than Texans living in the more arid western half of the state.

But what of the outliers, the sightings that have come in from drier areas? The reports from these more arid regions are so sporadic that any-

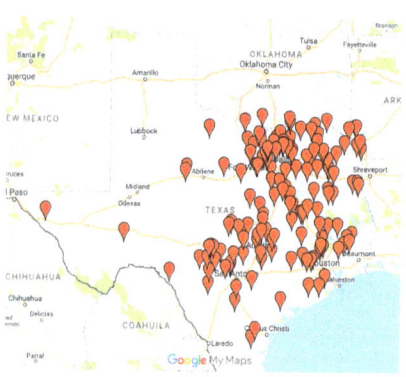

*Nearly all of the credible black panther sightings reported in Texas originate in the eastern half of the state (*Texas Cryptid Hunter)

thing offered here is pure speculation; however, many types of wildlife have a propensity to roam, and watercourses such as rivers and creeks would serve as ideal travel routes. Several of the more isolated westerly sightings have come from the upper reaches of some of Texas's major rivers such as the Brazos, Pecos, and Rio Grande. Perhaps the hunt for a mate or new territory drove these cats to these more lonesome and arid areas. Regardless, it would seem if this black panther mystery is going to be solved, the eastern half of Texas is as good a place as any to start.

While there is still a vast amount of sparsely populated land in the eastern half of Texas, and many sightings originate from these areas, a large number of sightings have been reported in shockingly urban environments. For example, I have received more black panther reports from Denton County, part of the Dallas-Fort Worth Metroplex, than any other county in Texas. Neighboring Collin County has been the source of multiple black panther reports as well and has also been quite the hot spot for sightings of mountain lions. This begs the question: Are big cats capable of living in close proximity to large population centers, possibly even within city limits, yet remain hidden? Some evidence suggests it could be possible.

It is a well-established fact that mountain lions have made homes within the city limits of large cities in southern California. Mountain lion P22, living in Los Angeles's Griffith Park, is probably the most well-

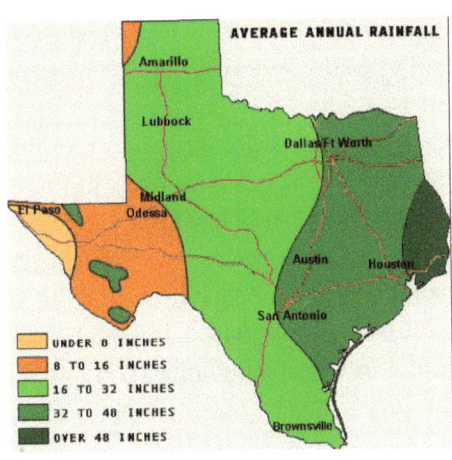

The majority of black panther sightings in Texas come from areas that receive a minimum of 32 inches of rainfall per year.

known case, but there are other examples of pumas residing in highly populated urban areas. In May of 2011, a mountain lion was shot and killed at a car wash in downtown El Paso.[47] Judging by video shot at the scene, this was a lean, lithe, and healthy cat and not a very old or sick animal that wandered into town out of desperation. In May of 2012, a female puma was spotted trotting down Arizona Avenue in downtown Santa Monica, California. Officers attempted to sedate the big cat using tranquilizer darts, but the drugs had no effect. At that point, officials had little choice and shot the 100-lb. cat.[48] Closer to home, a mountain lion was spotted multiple times in and around the village of Salado, Texas, in the spring of 2017. Things reached a crescendo when a deer kill was found cached in a brushy area near a playground on the property of the First Baptist Church. A blood trail and clear drag marks were evident at the scene that confirmed the identity of the predator.[49] Other major metropolitan areas that have been visited by mountain lions include Reno, Denver, and Santa Cruz.

While these incidents did take place in urban areas, they are all located in the western or southwestern United States. Have any large cats been spotted in large population centers in the Midwest or eastern portion of the U.S.? The answer is yes. In April of 2008, a cougar was shot and killed in Chicago, the nation's third most populous city.[50] The question as to whether this cat was truly wild or an escaped or released pet was never satisfactorily answered. There have also been reported sightings in Wisconsin, Ohio, and Missouri. Farther to the east, cougars have been spotted in urban centers in Delaware, Pennsylvania, Connecticut, Washington D.C., and New York.

The explanation most often given by wildlife officials concerning these urban mountain lion sightings is that the cats were likely just passing through and not actually living in the cities. This is not an illogical assumption, as many of the largest cities are built on or near watercourses with substantial riparian areas bordering them. As has been established, all manner of wildlife use watercourses as travel routes. It is not hard to picture a big cat traveling one of these routes and finding its way into the city limits.

Still, the possibility of truly urban big cats is intriguing. According to a joint study conducted by the University of California at Los Angeles and the National Parks Service, at least some predatory cats hunt in, or very near, developed areas on a regular basis. The study found that female mountain lions are most likely to hunt near town and often take prey less than one mile from developed areas. Researchers theorized that this behavior could be an effort to avoid the more territorial and aggressive male mountain lions roaming the wilder areas of Southern California.[51] Could these same circumstances be driving female mountain lions closer to developed areas in other parts of the country, too?

Cougars, similar to this one, were spotted in urban areas of Collin and Denton Counties (Texas) in the summer of 2014. (USFWS|Wikipedia Commons)

There is evidence to suggest that big cats may be able to thrive in human-dominated areas under other conditions as well. In 2014, the Wildlife Conservation Society (WCS) published the first ever GPS-based study of leopards in India. The study revealed some of the secrets of these furtive cats. The study focused on five leopards deemed "problem animals" that were captured in human-dominated areas. None of the leopards that were captured had been involved in any sort of predatory attack on people, but authorities felt their presence was a risk to the local population. The five leopards (two males and three females) were radio collared so that their movements could be tracked. Two of the cats were transported and released approximately 30 miles from their capture site, while the other three were released near the site of their capture.

The researchers monitored the leopards for over a year and observed several interesting behaviors. For example, the two leopards that were moved the farthest from their capture site immediately began traveling away from their area of relocation. One cat moved 55 miles over the course of the study, while the second moved 28 miles. This seemed to indicate that the common practice of relocating problem animals might be a waste of time and money. The co-author of the study, Vidya Athreya of WCS India said, "This indicated the futility of translocation as a management strategy; this could have, in fact, aggravated the conflict, as these animals passed through highly human-dominated (even industrial) areas."

Also of interest was how the leopards adopted strategies to avoid human contact, despite the fact they had become dependent upon resources (inadvertently) provided by them. The study revealed the animals moved at night, which minimized the chances of encountering humans. The cats were quite bold, sometimes approaching within 82-feet of human habitations. It became obvious that the cats were not interested in the humans in these areas; rather, this proximity to civilization allowed them to prey upon livestock at night with little risk of being seen. The study confirmed that these cats were residents within these human population centers and not transients.

One final interesting note was the discovery that the home ranges of the three leopards living in the areas of highest human density are the smallest ranges ever recorded – 3 to 5.7 square miles – for leopards anywhere in the world. "The home ranges of the three animals are comparable to those in highly productive protected areas with a very good prey density," said Athreya. "This indicated that food sources associated with humans (domestic animals) supported these leopards."

To summarize, these leopards not only survived, they thrived within the confines of human population centers. Two of the females even gave birth during the study. The leopards were permanent residents of these highly-populated areas and were not just transients passing through on their way to another location. Despite their proximity to people, none of the leopards in the study were involved in any attacks on humans prior to capture or following release and were rarely seen.[52] So, it seems there are at least two species of large, long-tailed cat in the world that have developed the ability to survive quite nicely near, and even in, human population centers.

I have always felt the idea of big cats of one species or another taking up residence in large cities was not as outlandish as many think. Many large cities have areas that are all but deserted. These areas might have once been industrial areas or residential neighborhoods but are now overgrown, untended, and neglected areas shunned by most humans. These areas often become the homes of feral cats and dogs, coyotes, and bobcats. Why could a larger predator not also find a way to survive in such an area? The prey base would likely consist of said feral cats and dogs and opossums along with rodents ranging from mice and rats to rabbits. A cat that moved about mostly between the hours of dusk and dawn could likely avoid detection for long periods of time.

In summary, vast tracts of forests and wilderness still exist in Texas and the American South. These areas could easily support a breeding population of big cats. In addition, anecdotal evidence, both in the United States and Asia, suggests, whether by choice or necessity, that big cats may be in the process of successfully adapting to living in much closer proximity to large human population centers than anyone thought possible only a few years ago. This fact calls into serious question the theory that fragmented forests and urban sprawl prevent populations of big cats from becoming established.

Finally, the undeniable correlation between annual precipitation rates and black panther sightings are indicative that there is likely a biological entity of some kind responsible for the sightings of large, black, long-tailed cats in Texas, and that the phenomenon is not some sort of mass hysteria or hoax.

5

Zeroing In

THE 148 CREDIBLE SIGHTINGS of large, black, long-tailed cats I've charted come from 83 of Texas's 254 counties (33%). My hope was that by charting individual sightings, the best areas on which to zero in on these cryptid cats would reveal themselves. Perhaps clusters of sightings, or some other pattern, would become apparent. I believe that is exactly what has happened.

First, a bit of a broad view. As previously mentioned, the bulk of these sightings occurred in the eastern half of the state. As the individual reports were added to the distribution map, an obvious correlation between the location of the sightings and average annual rainfall became obvious. The majority of sightings have taken place in areas that receive, on average, 32-48+ inches of precipitation per year. The correlation is very strong and is illustrated clearly when a map showing annual rainfall in Texas is compared to a map showing the counties where black panther sightings have been reported.

At first glance, it might appear that there are a significant number of outliers: sightings that have taken place in drier more arid climates. A closer look reveals this really is not the case. Take, for example, the sightings that have been charted west of San Antonio. Most assume this is a dry and desert-like area that would receive far less than 32 inches of rainfall per year; however, a close look at the precipitation map shows the dark green area that represents 32-48 inches of annual rainfall bows westward in this exact location. This fact keeps these southern Hill Country sightings very much in line with the rainfall hypothesis.

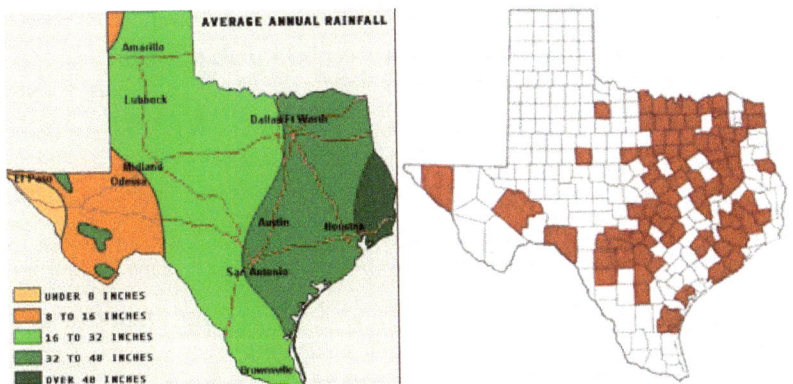

The majority of black panther sightings have taken place in areas that receive more than 32 inches of rainfall per year.
(Texas Cryptid Hunter)

Another seeming outlier would be the sightings in Pecos and Hudspeth Counties in far west Texas. Most people know that the Trans-Pecos region, including the Big Bend country, is very dry. For the most part that is true, but an examination of the precipitation map brings yet another surprise. Even within this dry and arid region of Texas, there are pockets of land that receive 32-48 inches of rainfall per year on average. While the sightings in these areas may not have taken place in those exact pockets indicated on the precipitation map, they did occur nearby. This, in my opinion, keeps these sightings in line with the rainfall correlation theory as well.

The idea that water is key when it comes to where these enigmatic cats might be found can be taken a bit further if we move beyond simply average annual rainfall and look at how many sightings have taken place in close proximity to major Texas rivers. Even the sightings that appear out of place and far from other reported incidents, such as those that have taken place in Knox and Nolan Counties, actually fit this narrative quite well, as both counties sit near the headwaters of the Brazos River.

All of the other sightings on the map fit this scenario as well, as the eastern half of Texas is incredibly rich in water resources. Major and minor rivers, creeks, streams, and bayous wind through the region, making water easily accessible. These waterways often cut through dense forests or are lined on both sides by riparian greenbelts making them ideal travel corridors for all manner of wildlife. The cover provided would make it possible for a big cat to move about with virtually no chance of being seen by humans.

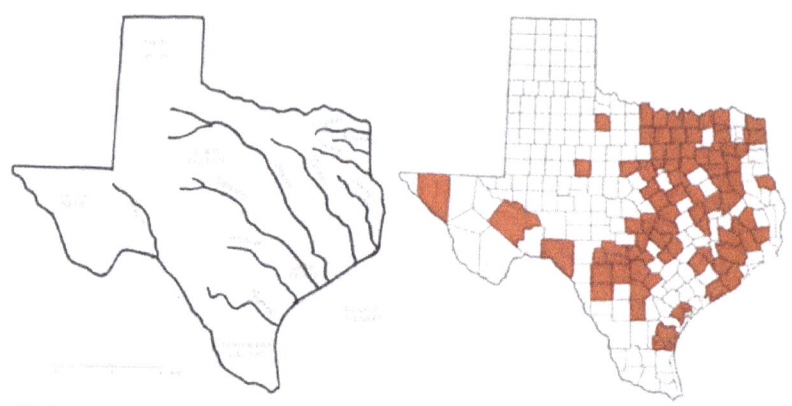

Sightings of black panthers, almost without exception, have occurred near one of the major rivers of Texas. (Texas Cryptid Hunter)

So the sighting distribution would seem to indicate there is a biological entity of some kind responsible for the black panther sightings in Texas. The fact that most sightings occur in areas that receive 32-48+ inches of rainfall per year and in close proximity to major rivers or waterways seems to mirror the behavior one would expect from not only a big cat of some kind, but most types of wildlife.

Another factor that leads me to believe there is a living, breathing animal responsible for these sightings is the continuity of reports from county to county. Upon examination of the map of Texas counties, it becomes clear that these sightings are not taking place in isolation. The counties where black panther sightings have occurred are nearly contiguous. They almost all share a border with another county from which sighting reports have come. It is easy to see just how few islands — counties where sightings have taken place but that do not share a border with at least one other county that has done likewise — there are within the state. A close look at these few islands reveals that nearly all of them are no more than one county away from other sighting reports. This might indicate that these cryptid cats are present in the buffer county but just have not been reported to me yet.

The handful of isolated counties more than one county away from other sighting locations are found in the western half of the state. These counties are, for the most part, sparsely populated. This lack of human presence could account for the dearth of sightings; even so, these lonesome regions are no more than two counties from other sighting locations. In my mind, this is yet another indicator that there is a biological entity behind the black panther sightings in Texas. It stands to reason that if sightings of black panthers were only the result of hoaxers playing tricks, misidentifications, or hallucinations, the distribution of these incidents would be much less concentrated. The sightings would be all over the state and exhibit no real rhyme or reason.

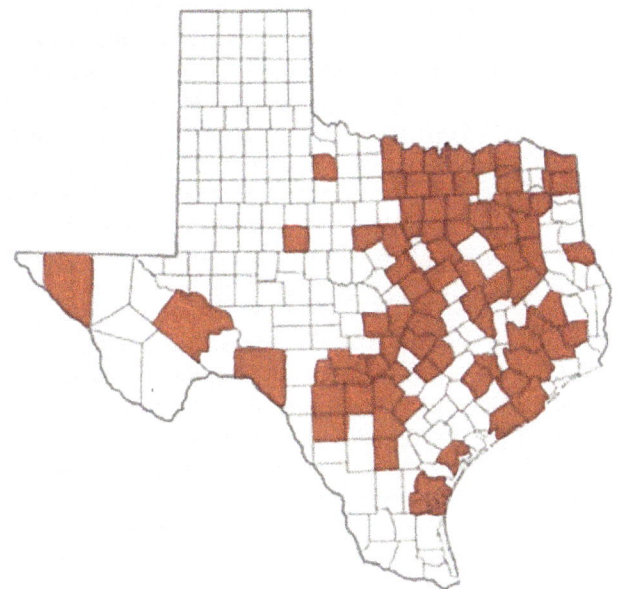

*The dark areas represent counties in which black panther sightings have occurred. Note how many counties with sightings share a border with other counties with similar reports. (*Texas Cryptid Hunter*)*

It now seems obvious that the best chance of seeing one of these large, black, long-tailed cats would be to stake out a county in the eastern half of the state. Narrowing it down a bit more, the search should likely be conducted in counties that either abut a major river or have a major waterway running through them. There are, however, many Texas counties that fit this criterion. Can we narrow the search area even more? I believe so. Some counties have produced more sighting reports than others. At the end of this chapter is a comprehensive breakdown of the number of black panther sightings by county in the Lone Star State. The figures were accurate as of August 3, 2017. I believe the data included on this Sightings by County chart might help us further zero in on these phantom cats.

It should now be clear that there is an ample amount of wooded and/or lightly populated land in the American South to sustain a breeding population of big cats. Jaguars once ranged from the Pacific Northwest as far east as what is now Pennsylvania. Mountain lions once ranged across the entire North American continent. Why could a similarly sized species of cat, in limited numbers, not manage to do the same today? I also believe that data collected on these sightings strongly indicates a biological basis behind the sightings of black panthers, at least in Texas. The distribution of sightings is exactly what would be expected of a large predatory cat living in the Lone Star State.

Even the skeptic might begrudgingly admit at this point that there is enough room for a predatory cat to roam in Texas and the American South, and that the distribution of sightings seems to be what one would expect from a living species. But that does not change the fact that there is no such thing as a black panther. So if there is a real animal out there responsible for these sightings, what could it be? What is roaming around out there?

Black Panther Sightings by County in Texas[53]

Anderson - 2
Andrews -
Angelina -
Aransas -
Archer -
Armstrong -
Atascosa - 1
Austin - 1
Bailey -
Bandera - 2
Bastrop - 2
Baylor -
Bee -
Bell - 2
Bexar - 2
Blanco - 1
Borden -
Bosque -
Bowie - 3
Brazoria - 1
Brazos - 1
Brewster -
Briscoe -
Brooks -
Brown -
Burleson -
Burnet - 2
Caldwell - 2
Calhoun -
Callahan -
Cameron -
Camp -
Carson -
Cass - 3
Castro -
Chambers -
Cherokee - 2
Childress -
Clay - 1
Cochran -
Coke -
Coleman -
Collin - 3
Collingsworth -
Colorado - 1
Comal - 1
Comanche -
Concho -
Cooke -
Coryell - 1
Cottle -
Crane -
Crockett -
Crosby -
Culberson -
Dallam -
Dallas - 2
Dawson -
De Witt -
Deaf Smith -
Delta - 1
Denton - 8
Dickens -
Dimmit -
Donley -
Duval -
Eastland - 1
Ector -
Edwards -
Ellis - 1
El Paso -
Erath - 1
Falls -
Fannin - 2
Fayette -
Fisher -
Floyd -
Foard -
Fort Bend - 3
Franklin -
Freestone -
Frio -
Gaines -
Galveston -
Garza -
Gillespie -
Glasscock -
Goliad -
Gonzales -
Gray -
Grayson - 2
Gregg -
Grimes -
Guadalupe -
Hale -
Hall -
Hamilton - 1
Hansford -
Hardeman -
Hardin - 3
Harris -
Harrison - 3
Hartley -
Haskell -
Hays -
Hemphill -
Henderson - 1
Hidalgo -
Hill - 4
Hockley -
Hood - 2
Hopkins - 1
Houston - 1
Howard -
Hudspeth - 1
Hunt -
Hutchinson -
Irion -
Jack - 1
Jackson -
Jasper -
Jeff Davis -
Jefferson -
Jim Hogg -
Jim Wells -
Johnson - 1
Jones -
Karnes -
Kaufman - 1
Kendall - 1
Kenedy -
Kent -
Kerr - 4
Kimble -
King -
Kinney -
Kleberg - 1
Knox - 1
La Salle -
Lamar - 2
Lamb -
Lampasas -
Lavaca -
Lee - 1
Leon - 3
Liberty - 2
Limestone - 2
Lipscomb -
Live Oak -
Llano - 3
Loving -
Lubbock -
Lynn -
Madison -
Marion -
Martin -
Mason -
Matagorda - 2
Maverick -
McCulloch -
McLennan - 1
McMullen - 1
Medina - 1
Menard - 1
Midland -
Milam -
Mills -
Mitchell -
Montague - 1
Montgomery - 1
Moore -
Morris - 1
Motley -
Nacogdoches -
Navarro -
Newton -
Nolan - 2
Nueces - 1
Ochiltree -
Oldham -
Orange -
Palo Pinto -
Panola -

Parker - 3   Rusk -   Sutton -   Victoria -   Young -
Parmer -   Sabine -   Swisher -   Walker - 1   Zapata -
Pecos - 1   San Augustine -   Tarrant - 5   Waller -   Zavala -
Polk - 1   San Jacinto - 1   Taylor -   Ward -
Potter -   San Patricio -   Terrell -   Washington -
Presidio -   San Saba -   Terry -   Webb -
Rains - 1   Schleicher -   Throckmorton -   Wharton -
Randall -   Scurry -   Titus -   Wheeler -
Reagan -   Shackelford -   Tom Green -   Wichita -
Real - 1   Shelby - 3   Travis - 2   Wilbarger -
Red River -   Sherman -   Trinity -   Willacy -
Reeves -   Smith - 3   Tyler -   Williamson - 2
Refugio - 1   Somervell -   Upshur - 1   Wilson - 1
Roberts -   Starr -   Upton -   Winkler -
Robertson - 2   Stephens -   Uvalde - 1   Wise - 4
Rockwall - 1   Sterling -   Val Verde - 1   Wood - 3
Runnels -   Stonewall -   Van Zandt - 3   Yoakum -

6

The Suspects: Jaguar

MAINSTREAM SCIENTISTS and laymen alike find it difficult to believe that a species of cat consistently estimated to weigh between 50 and 150 pounds could have been roaming the Lone Star State for the last 200 years or so and remained undocumented. Skeptics simply feel it would be impossible for a species of this size to have remained undiscovered for so long. While it can be argued that new species are discovered all the time, including some that are large, those tend to be found in remote and exotic locales like the Amazon rainforest, the jungles of Southeast Asia, and the Congo of Africa and not in the thoroughly explored and developed lands of Texas or the American South. While I do not completely agree with this line of thinking, it is understandable. If any of the reports of black panthers made by the people of Texas are deemed credible, and an undocumented species of cat is thought to be at best unlikely and at worst impossible, that leaves us with only known animals as the culprits behind the sightings. This begs the question: Are there any cats native to Texas that could be misidentified as black panthers? The short answer is yes, and the first such suspect on our list is the jaguar.

The jaguar (*Panthera onca*) does exhibit melanism and once roamed freely all over the land that would become Texas. In fact, the range of the jaguar was once quite extensive and included most of the North American continent. Jaguar fossils from the Pleistocene have been found as far to the northwest as Whitman County, Washington, and as far northeast as Port Kennedy, Pennsylvania.[54] In the southeast, jaguar fossils are among the most common of the large carnivores collected. In fact, jaguars may very well have been the most dominant carnivore of the Pleistocene in North American, more numerous even than the dire wolf or the legendary saber-toothed cat.⁵⁵

The jaguar is native to Texas and once roamed freely across most of the North American continent. (Henner Damke\Dreamstime.com)

A combination of factors led to the decline of jaguars in North America in ancient times. Many scholars believe the demise of the megafauna, most likely due to overhunting by indigenous peoples, had a direct impact on the jaguar population. Jaguars are large, robust cats and would have preyed on the various species of megafauna. Once these animals disappeared, it would have directly impacted the ability of jaguars to survive as the deer population was then much smaller than it is presently. The direct hunting of jaguars by native peoples, who prized their spotted coats, would have affected populations as well and driven these big cats to more lightly populated areas.

Despite these factors, there really is no reason that the jaguar could not have survived, albeit in limited numbers, into more recent times in its historical range. Some evidence suggests this may, indeed, be the case.

In 1958, a conch shell gorget (an engraved shell perforated for suspension and worn at the throat or chest) was unearthed in Benton County, Missouri, upon which the form of a jaguar was clearly engraved. The jaguar gorget is thought to have been created sometime between 250 B.C. and A.D. 450.[56] Similar engravings of jaguars were found on two bones unearthed from a Hopewell burial mound in Ohio, which dated to about 500 B.C. These engraved images do not prove that jaguars still existed in Missouri or Ohio between 500 B.C. and A.D. 450 but suggest it is a strong possibility.

Ancient artifacts are one thing; the first-hand observations of an early North American explorer are quite another. John Lawson was a wealthy 26-year-old man who decided to explore the Carolinas in 1700. Lawson's experiences and observations, collected along his 1,000-mile journey through North and South Carolina, were published in his book *A New Voyage to Carolina* in 1709. One account in the book seems to indicate the possibility that he observed a jaguar on his expedition.

> As we were on our road this morning, our Indian shot at a Tyger [sic], that cross'd our Way, he being a great distance from us. I believe he did him no harm, because he sat on his Breech afterwards, and look'd upon us. I suppose he expected to have had a Spaniel Bitch, that I had with me, for his breakfast, who run towards him, but Midway stopt her Career, and came sneaking back to us with her Tail betwixt her legs.[57]

Some scholars believe that Lawson misspoke when he called the cat in question a "tyger" and that he had really seen a mountain lion. Recall that the terms tyger, tiger, Mexican lion, and Mexican tiger were often used to describe jaguars from the 1700s to the early 1900s. Contextual evidence leads me to believe that Lawson knew the difference between the two species and did not err in the terminology used in his account. Another passage in his book would seem to support the idea that Lawson knew the difference between a jaguar, or tyger, and a mountain lion.

> Tygers are never met withal in the Settlement; but are more to the Westward, and are not numerous on this Side of the Chain of Mountains. I once saw one that was larger than a Panther* and seem'd to be a very bold Creature. The Indians that hunt in those Quarters, say, they are seldom met withal. It seems to differe [sic] from the Tyger of Asia and Africa.[58]

In this passage, Lawson clearly differentiates the size of the tyger from that of the panther, and where each species is most likely to be encountered. This seems to indicate that he was familiar with the more common mountain lion and that the tyger witnessed was something else entirely.

Of even more recent vintage is a newspaper account from the June 1886 edition of the *Donaldsonville Chief* that documents the killing of an "American tiger" weighing 250 lbs. and measuring 8-feet in length from the nose to the tip of the tail in Ascension Parish, Louisiana.[59] If accurate, this would mean jaguars were still living in Louisiana up until the very brink of the turn of the century.

Though the range of the jaguar in North America continued to shrink with every year that passed, a small population of these big cats did continue to make Texas their home even after disappearing from other regions of the country. The autobiography of Mrs. Otis McGaffey of Sabine Pass includes an account of her husband "killing a tiger cat" near the banks of the Sabine River as they returned from a trip to Natchitoches, Louisiana in 1841.[60] In an 1876 Beaumont, Texas, court case, William McFaddin swore that an acquaintance of his, one Absolom Williams, had been attacked by "a Bengal tiger that had escaped the circus" at his Hardin County log cabin in or about 1840.[61] Records, however, indicate that no circus reached that area of southeast Texas until 1881. If the basic story is factual, it is almost certain that what attacked Mr. Williams was a spotted jaguar.

---

* It should be noted here that the colloquial use of the term *panther* as a large, long-tailed, black cat did not take hold until Anglo settlers from the U.S. began pouring into what would become the American South in the late 1700s and early 1800s.

A series of articles written by Judge J.W. Moses, which appeared in a four-part series in the Sunday editions of the *San Antonio Express* in April of 1888, featured a run-in between a group of mustangers and a Mexican lion in or around 1850. In short, a group of cowboys encountered "el senor leon" in the chaparral of southwest Texas. The men ended up roping the unfortunate cat before dispatching it.[62] Four years later, the *Galveston Weekly News* published an article in February of 1892 documenting the buzz that was created when an east Texas local brought to authorities the scalp of an exceptionally large jaguar in the hopes of collecting a bounty on the predator. The article read in part, "Quite a curiosity was filed under Jasper County's Scalp Law recently, the head of an unusually large Mexican lion, which was killed in the lower section of the county by John Shepherd." According to the article, "The skull shows the head to be very nearly, if not equally, as large as an ordinary African lion's head."[63]

Jaguars persisted in the Big Thicket region of east Texas until the early 1900s and were occasionally encountered in the deep southern and far western portions of the state until 1948. That year, what is thought to have been the last two jaguars in Texas were killed. The first was dispatched along Santa Gertrudis Creek near Kingsville, and the second was killed near Highway 77.[64] That same year the government instituted a predator control program that poisoned animals on both sides of the U.S.-Mexico border. The program wiped out most of the big carnivores left along the Rio Grande, including Mexican grizzlies, most wolves, and any jaguars that might have survived to that point. Wildlife officials claim no jaguars have been seen in Texas since.

There is some anecdotal evidence that jaguars might not survive only in small numbers in the American South and Southwest but much farther north than anyone would have expected. Between 1991 and 2010, a study headed by Rick Rosatte, a senior research scientist for the Ontario Ministry of Natural Resources, was conducted in an effort to find out if wild cougars (*Puma concolor*) still roamed the rural areas of Ontario, Canada. The study was quite extensive and yielded 497 separate pieces of evidence indicating that cougars did, indeed, still exist in Ontario. Evidence collected included scat, hair, DNA, tracks, and photographs. In

The fact that jaguars do exhibit melanism on occasion makes them prime suspects in the black panther mystery. (Scheriton\Dreamstime.com)

addition, there were more than 470 sightings recorded, including some by highly qualified observers such as biologists. All of that is to make clear that this was no poorly organized, fly-by-night study; it was the real deal.

Interestingly, Rosatte documented sightings of not only the normal tawny-colored cougars but also many instances where "black cougars" or "black panthers" were seen. In all, the study cites 52 "credible" sightings of black cougars in Ontario between 1991 and 2010.[65] In addition, a clear photograph of a large black cat, matching the description given by many of the witnesses, was captured by one of the researcher's trail cameras. The photo is included in the published study but is described in an amazingly nonchalant manner. The caption to the photo states: "Photograph of a melanistic jaguar (*Panthera onca*) taken by a trail camera near Guelph, Ontario, in April 2010." Rosatte threw these sightings out and did not include them in the data published in the study: "Sightings that were identified by the observer as 'black cougars' or 'black panthers' were not included, as there are no records of a black phase of cougar occurring in North America. Credible black cougar sightings were assumed to be exotic cats such as a melanistic jaguar (*Panthera onca*) or a melanistic leopard (*Panthera pardus*)."⁶⁶ Rosatte cited a statement made by none other than the Texas Parks and Wildlife Department as the basis for this reasoning.

An image of what is believed to be a melanistic jaguar taken by trail camera near Guelph, Ontario in April of 2010. (Rick Rosatte)

Yet Rosatte himself described the sightings of "black cougars" or "black panthers" as credible. His team actually captured a photo backing up the claims of these "credible" witnesses but threw out the data and assumed all 52 sightings were glimpses of escaped exotic pets. Rosatte was certainly correct in pointing out that no black cougars had been documented. The fact that the accounts of 52 credible witnesses and one amazing photograph were, basically, dismissed and deemed unworthy of follow-up is, however, bothersome. Clearly, Rosatte's study was not an effort to prove the existence of black panthers. The purpose of the study was to find out if wild cougars had returned to Ontario. The study was wildly successfully in that regard, as the desired evidence was located and the answers sought were found. I cannot help but wonder, however, if the opportunity for an even greater discovery might have been overlooked when credible sightings of black panthers were ignored and the data discarded.

There are not many in the Lone Star State who would disagree with the official position that there are no jaguars in Texas, but there are some. It is true the majority of sighting reports I have received involved a large black cat of some kind, but reports of large spotted cats have occasionally come to my attention. Here are a few such reports I have collected over the years where the witness claims to have seen a very large, spotted cat. The reports that follow were actually posted on the *Smithsonian* website back in December of 2005 in response to an article titled "Return of the Jaguar?" by Will Rizzo.

> 2008
> My sons were in a creek in North Dallas this past June and two (age 22 and 24) of them saw a jaguar. City boys yes but these guys know their animals. It was about 30 feet across the creek and about 20 feet upstream, maybe 3:00 in the afternoon. They said it turned and saw them, and then eased on up into the brush. They were surprised by its lack of panic. They weren't about to follow. This sounds strange but they were positive it was a jaguar. — Steve
>
> 2010
> Back in 1989, when I was 15 years old my family and I made a fishing trip to Falcon Lake in South Texas. As we left our campsite to go to the nearby town for supplies we encountered a large cat about 30 yards in front of us. My father stopped the car as we watched it cross the dirt road. We couldn't believe it because it was spotted like a jaguar but we believed that it was almost impossible to have actually seen one since they were known to be long gone from

Texas. As we drove past the place where it had crossed we rolled up our windows thinking it could come out of the brush and try to attack us but of course it had disappeared. When we arrived at the local supermarket my father told the store manager what we had seen and they said that they were somewhat common in the area and had been sighted for years. That experience is something that I would never forget and, to say the least, we spent the rest of our trip sleeping in the car instead of the tent. As an adult I have returned to the lake with my own kids and ask the locals about any big cats in the area and they all mentioned that jaguars haven't been seen for over 15 years but do get a lot of mountain lion sightings. Well, I thought I'd share my big cat story with you. — Josh

2011
A few years ago my uncle and I had a 25,000 acre hunting lease on the Rio Grande river near Laredo, Texas. We observed a large Jaguar on the Texas side of the river, heard its distinctive grunts, and found its tracks. In addition, we saw a mountain lion and found its tracks. There is such a large difference between the two animals, that mistaken identity is impossible. — Bobby

While most of the alleged jaguar sightings in Texas have been, as might be expected, near the Mexican border, there are some notable exceptions. The first report related above would be one; the following two accounts would be others. The message below was related to me in February of 2014 and originally posted on the *Texas Cryptid Hunter* website:

I have seen a spotted cat in Texas. I saw it almost every day for about 2 weeks then it was gone. As I have looked into big cats I have found they move around as the food does and I know that what I saw was a jag and they have been here for over 75 years as I talk to the old cowboys around Quanah, Texas.[67] — Name withheld by author

Quanah, Texas, is located right at the base of the Texas Panhandle just south of the Red River and more than 500 miles due north of the Rio Grande River, which forms the border between the United States and Mexico. If this gentleman really did see a jaguar, it was a long way from home. I found the account especially interesting as it followed on the heels of another anecdote that had recently been shared with me that allegedly took place only 150 miles or so from the Texas Panhandle town of Pampa. In the interest of full disclosure, the following incident was related to me second-hand and after-the-fact. I cannot provide any documentation on the incident; however, the person who shared it with me is a man of impeccable character I know very well and for whom I have the highest regard. I have absolutely no doubt he told me the story exactly as it was related to him.

He told me that a rancher from the Panhandle – a friend of his – made regular reports to the Texas Parks and Wildlife Department several years ago regarding the loss of large livestock, including alpacas. After the rancher reported the killing of a second alpaca in a month, the game warden came out to take a look around. Together, the pair started a tour of the property in the hopes of coming across tracks, scat, or other spoor that might identify the predator. They had not been looking long before finding the hindquarters of the alpaca 20-feet up in a tree that was part of a greenbelt paralleling a creek running through the property. According to my acquaintance, the game warden told the rancher that this was not a cougar and that he likely had a jaguar on the property. He was warned to arm himself, be very aware of his surroundings at all times, and to avoid going out on the property at night if at all possible. The cat was never seen and eventually must have moved on as the killings stopped shortly thereafter. The rancher and my friend remain in touch and to date he has had no more problems along these lines.[68]

There are some possible issues with this story: most notably, jaguars are not known to cache kills in trees. This behavior is most often seen in leopards, particularly in Africa, where kills can be taken away from them by bigger, stronger, and more numerous predators such as lions and hyenas. Jaguars are the apex predator wherever they roam. There would simply be no reason to cache a kill in a tree as no other predator is large enough or numerous enough to snatch a carcass away with the possible exception being a pack of coyotes. In any case, my friend is adamant the game warden used the term jaguar. While I cannot provide documentation to back up this account, I felt it interesting enough to include here.

It is true that these accounts do not prove jaguars still prowl the Lone Star State; however, they are powerful anecdotal evidence that the existence of a small population of these big cats is a distinct possibility. The argument for this being the case is only strengthened by the fact that jaguars have recently been photographed in Arizona. In 1996, Warner Glenn, a rancher and guide from Douglas, was out on a mountain lion hunt in the Peloncillo Mountains of southeastern Arizona when his dogs caught a scent and were off. When Glenn caught up to the pack, he found that his hounds had not treed a mountain lion but, instead, a jaguar. Glenn took some photos and then pulled his dogs off the cat and allowed it to escape.[69] Six months later, a second jaguar was treed by two hunters just 150 miles west of the spot where the Glenn encounter took place. This led to the placing of game cameras in the area in 1999. It took a while, but in December of 2001, a male jaguar dubbed Macho A was photographed. Macho A was photographed several times over the next two years. A second male, Macho B, was photographed next, followed by a possible third jaguar that researchers hoped was a female.

Macho B became something of a celebrity when he was captured in a trap set by the Arizona Game and Fish Department. According to Arizona wildlife officials, the trap was intended for black bear and/or mountain lions and was being used to survey these two species south of Tucson. Though very old at an estimated 15-16 years, Macho B was deemed healthy and fitted with a lightweight satellite tracking collar in the hopes that the data gained would reveal more about jaguar habits in Arizona. This was not to be, however, as the data soon revealed that Macho B was anything but healthy. Tracking information revealed a continuously diminishing range, and officials decided to recapture the jaguar in order to determine what was wrong. According to Arizona wildlife officials, Macho B was found to have terminal kidney failure – not unusual for a cat his age – and euthanized.

The claims of the accidental capture and the reasons for putting Macho B down took a hit when it was discovered the bear trap in which the jaguar had been captured had been baited with female jaguar scat. In addition, it was discovered that the cat had not been put down due to failing kidneys; rather, it was because Macho B never recovered from injuries he sustained in the trap or the effects of the tranquilizer used initially to sedate him.[70] The whole sorry affair ended up with the conviction of one biologist and severely damaged reputations for others.

An image of Macho B, one of the male jaguars seen in Arizona in recent years. If jaguars are crossing into Arizona from Mexico, what would prevent the same scenario from occurring in Texas? (Arizona Game and Fish Department)

While the decision to put Macho B down was controversial, and possibly criminal in nature, the episode did rally jaguar proponents and conservationists into action. Predictably, years of legal wrangling ensued, but eventually 1,309 square miles across southern Arizona and a small part of southern New Mexico were designated as prime jaguar habitat and essential for the survival of this endangered big cat. The designated land includes mountain ranges in rural Prima, Cochise, and Santa Cruz counties in Arizona, and portions of Hidalgo County in New Mexico.

These are areas known to have been occupied by jaguars, at least on occasion, since 1962 and meet the government's criteria of having rugged terrain, expansive open spaces, availability of surface water, an adequate prey base, minimal human presence, relatively easy access to northern Mexico, and be 3%-40% covered by Madrean woodlands including oak, juniper, and pine or by semi-desert grasslands.[71] The bottom line here is that jaguars are crossing the border from northern Mexico into Arizona and New Mexico; there is simply no reason to think they could not be roaming into Texas as well.

If jaguars are moving into Texas, at least occasionally, they could be responsible for some of the black panther sightings reported in the Lone Star State as the species does exhibit melanism. It is impossible to say exactly what percentage of jaguars exhibit melanism, but it is generally accepted that the condition occurs in 6%-10% of wild specimens. While these percentages represent a significant number of jaguars, black specimens remain solidly in the minority. Many who argue against the jaguar as a possible candidate for the black panther of Texas point to the fact that up to 10% of the population may be melanistic, but that leaves 90% of the population that is normally colored and marked. If jaguars are still roaming Texas, witnesses should be seeing the golden-colored, spotted cats roughly nine times more often than melanistic cats. Where are the normal-colored, spotted jaguars?

The question is valid and the fact that so few Texans have reported spotted cats would seem to eliminate the jaguar as a suspect in this mystery; however, a little research on basic genetics seems to indicate that crossing the jaguar off the black panther suspect list may be premature. Melanism in felines can be a result of either a dominant gene mutation or a recessive gene mutation. The difference between the two types of mutations is significant and is the reason the jaguar has to remain on the list of black panther suspects (The topic of melanism will be discussed in more detail in Chapter 11).

In summary, the jaguar is native to Texas, does exhibit melanism, has been documented in other states bordering Mexico, and generally fits the description of size and weight reported by many people who claim to have witnessed a black panther. While it is unlikely melanistic jaguars can explain all the black panther sightings reported in Texas, the largest cat in the Americas must remain a prime suspect in this mystery.

7

The Suspects: Cougar

IT IS UNIVERSALLY ACCEPTED that Texas is home to one big cat, which, other than coloration, fits the description given by most witnesses who claim to have seen a black panther. The mountain lion or cougar (*Puma concolor*) is considered uncommon, certainly, but hardly rare. The Texas Parks and Wildlife Department, along with most distribution maps, claim that breeding populations of cougars are limited almost exclusively to the far west Trans-Pecos region of the Lone Star State and deep south Texas near the border of Mexico along the Rio Grande River. They do admit that the species is now being seen in the Hill Country and "in more counties than they were 10 years ago and appear to be expanding their range into Central Texas."[72]

Cougars range from Canada to Patagonia and, other than their color, fit the general description (size and shape) given by witnesses who claim to have seen black panthers. (Twildlife/Dreamstime.com)

I can attest to this expanding range as I witnessed a mountain lion crossing a forest service road in May of 2005. The incident took place near Stubblefield Lake in the Sam Houston National Forest. The cat was very long and low to the ground. It was a honey-blonde color with a white throat and muzzle. The tail was very long. After reporting my visual to a forest ranger, I was told I was likely mistaken and had seen a bobcat. "There are no mountain lions in these woods," he said. When I told him that I respectfully disagreed, he merely shrugged his shoulders. Due to the size of this species, the historically large area of distribution, contemporary sightings, my own visual, and its seemingly expanding modern range, the cougar must be considered as a prime suspect in the black panther mystery.

The cougar has the widest distribution of any wildcat on the planet. The range of this cat stretches from Canada to the southernmost region of South America.[73] Due to this wide distribution, the cougar is known by many different names. Mountain lion, puma, catamount, mountain screamer, and painter are but a few of the regional names for this cat. The term painter is especially interesting. Some experts feel it is merely the way some with regional accents/dialects pronounced the word panther, while other lexicographers regard it as a variant used in the southern United States meant to differentiate between the common tawny-colored cougar (painter) and the large black cats (panthers) living in the same areas. This matches up with my own experiences, as most in east Texas and the South use the term panther only when describing a large, long-tailed black cat. Again, the exception to this rule is in the state of Florida where the Florida panther is a well-known endangered species.

Cougars are the fourth largest cat on the planet behind the tiger, African lion, and jaguar. Because of this, many consider them one of the "big cats." Technically, the cougar should be considered the largest of the small cats as they belong to the subfamily *Felinae*, not the subfamily *Pantherinae*.[74] They stand, on average, between 24-35 inches at the shoulder and measure between 6.5-7.9 feet long from nose to the tail tip when fully grown. They are powerful and robust cats that can weigh in excess of 200 lbs.[75] The tail is long, typically one-third of the body length, and helps with balance while jumping or climbing. Cougars range in color from the typical honey-tawny color to various shades of brown and even gray. The belly and chest are often much lighter than the dorsal area with a cream color or white being most common.

There has never been a documented specimen of a melanistic cougar. This is undeniable fact; however, rumors and legends abound regarding the possible existence of black pumas. A few enigmatic photos exist, and there are some intriguing descriptions of what might have been black cougars given by European explorers and adventurers in the 1800s, but there is no hard proof. Once again, we are left to consider anecdotal evidence only.

One such interesting piece of anecdotal evidence comes from none other than Laura Ingalls Wilder, author of the well-known Little House books. In this series of books, Ingalls Wilder recalls her youth on the American frontier in the 1870s. The first book in the series, titled *Little House in the Big Woods*, features a memory of Laura's where her father tells her a story about how her grandfather nearly fell prey to a huge black panther in the Big Woods of Wisconsin years before. (The tale can be found in Chapter 2 of the book.) In the story, Ingalls Wilder's grandpa was returning to his homestead from town. He was later than he would have liked and darkness had fallen. Suddenly, he heard a panther scream. The scream was described as being like that of a woman. Frightened, Grandpa kicked his horse into a full gallop. The terrified animal did not need much encouragement, as the panther was in hot pursuit. Ingalls Wilder writes that the cat was "a huge, black panther" with "enormous slashing claws and long sharp teeth." Ingalls concludes the story with this passage:

> At last the horse ran up to Grandpa's house. Grandpa saw the panther springing. Grandpa jumped off the horse, against the door. He burst through the door and slammed it behind him. The panther landed on the horse's back, just where Grandpa had been.
>
> The horse screamed terribly, and ran. He was running away into the Big Woods, with the panther riding on

his back and ripping his back with its claws. But Grandpa grabbed his gun from the wall and got to the window, just in time to shoot the panther dead.

Grandpa said he would never again go into the Big Woods without his gun.[76]

While it is universally acknowledged that the Little House books are autobiographical in nature and based on the childhood memories Ingalls Wilder had of growing up in the Big Woods near Pepin, Wisconsin, there is no way of knowing for sure if "The Story of Grandpa and the Black Panther" was factual. What is important for our purposes is that Laura Ingalls Wilder was fully aware of the supposed existence of these animals as early as the late 1920s – early 1930s when the book was being written and published. It is highly unlikely, in my opinion, that Ingalls Wilder just dreamed up the idea of a ferocious, large, black, long-tailed cat for her book. Whether she really did hear this story from her father as a young girl, or added it to her book to entertain her readers, is irrelevant. What is relevant is that she knew what black panthers were and that they were, allegedly, out there.

I have included the Ingalls Wilder passage in this chapter due to her description of how the panther sounded when it screamed. "It sounded like a woman" is something I have heard time and time again and is, I believe, an important clue. As stated previously, cougars are not true big cats. One reason they are not designated as such is that they are unable to roar. They lack the larynx and hyoid structure of the genus *Panthera*, making roaring impossible. Cougars are capable, however, of making a wide variety of sounds such as hisses, growls, and purring.[77] Some have even reported hearing cougars make a whistling noise.

The vocalization for which they are best known, however, is their scream. It is most often described as sounding like a woman screaming out of terror or pain, and can be quite unnerving when heard in the wild. This scream is described to a T by Charles Ingalls as he relates the frightening encounter of his father years before. If the story of Grandpa Ingalls's encounter with a black panther back in the 1800s is true, and if the panther really did produce a scream like that of a woman, then the cat in question was likely a cougar and not a melanistic jaguar.

This woman-like screaming of which Ingalls Wilder wrote is not unique to Wisconsin. It is a sound that has been reported by many Texans, particularly in the Big Thicket region, and associated with cougars and black panthers for decades. East Texas newsman Archie Fullingim was the editor, printer, and publisher of the *The Kountze News* for years and wrote about anything and everything that occurred in and around the Big Thicket, including run-ins with black panthers. Here are excerpts from several columns in which he discusses not only black panther sightings, but also the woman-like screams so often associated with these enigmatic cats:

> Periodically in Hardin County there rage in the columns of *The Kountze News* ... vitriolic word battles over whether or not a panther screams like a woman. Somebody will come in and say that he saw a panther in the Thicket (and it's always a black panther), and he will say that it screamed like a hysterical, frightened woman.[78]
>
> "As I say, this happens two or three times a year. Always it gets a rise out of panther experts in Dallas, Houston, Beaumont, Wyoming, and Arizona, who send in long letters – backed, of course, by the *National Geographic* magazine and encyclopedias – arguing that there is no such thing as a black panther, and that a panther never, never screams, especially like a fear-crazed woman.[79]
>
> In the Big Thicket country old-timers are convinced that when someone died in the old days and was laid out in the residence to await burial, a black panther would always mount the gatepost and scream bloody murder like a woman...
>
> Nearly everybody in the Big Thicket fervently believes that panthers may be tawny in color every other place, but that in the Big Thicket they are coal black with scarlet

mouths and scarlet tongues, and with eyes that shine in the dark. They also believe that panthers scream like a woman, and you can find hundreds of people who have heard panthers scream.[80]

If there is a large cat of some kind roaming the Big Thicket region of Texas, and if it screams as has been described, it is not a jaguar; it is a cougar. This would not seem to be reconcilable with the physical description of a coal black cat, however, as no specimen of a melanistic puma has ever been obtained. While this is true, it is not exactly accurate to say a black puma has never been described by experts in the field of wildlife.

Georges-Louis Leclerc, Comte de Buffon, was an influential French naturalist who published 36 volumes of his *Histoire Naturelle* during his lifetime. He was so prodigious that additional volumes were published from his notes after his death. In his *Histoire Naturelle*, de Buffon described a large cat from South America that sounds very much like it could have been a black cougar. He dubbed this melanistic felid the *cougar noire*.[81] Many are of the opinion that de Buffon was merely describing a melanistic jaguar; however, the description given of the cat in question does not seem to match what would be seen in a jaguar. The characteristics described by de Buffon, his contemporary, Thomas Pennant, and other naturalists who followed them, was that the dorsal surfaces of the *cougar noire* were covered with short, black, glossy hairs. The underside of the cat was much lighter with the inside of the legs, throat, and belly all appearing whitish.

Was the *cougar noire* truly a black cougar? Since no specimens are known to have been taken, we will likely never know. Still, the accounts of de Buffon, Pennant, and others should not be taken lightly. These men, while not infallible, were the giants in their field at the time. They were not rank amateurs who believed anything and everything they heard. They would have required some hard evidence to include this cat in their documentation efforts.

For years, a rumor has circulated saying that a black cougar was shot in Brazil by a hunter named William Thomson in 1843. Thomson allegedly killed the cat in the Carandahy River region. Unfortunately, the skin of this cat was not kept and the specimen has been lost. Thomson did, however, give a description of this unique cougar in his book *Great Cats I Have Known* (1896). He wrote: "The whole head, back, and sides, and even the tail were glossy black, while the throat, belly, and inner surfaces of the legs, were shaded off to a stone gray."[82] If true, this could have been the *cougar noire* described by de Buffon years before. Yet again, a potential game changing specimen was lost before being properly examined.

Historical accounts are one thing; photographic evidence is another entirely. Are there any photos out there showing black cougars? Possibly. There is one old and well-circulated photo that seems to show a black cougar. The photo has really made the rounds since the advent of the internet, and proponents of the melanistic cougar theory regarding the black panther mystery often point to it as proof that such a cat exists.

The photo in question was taken in Costa Rica in 1959 and features a dead cougar strung up and hanging by its back feet from a tree. A local is standing next to the specimen to provide scale, or so I am guessing. The cougar was shot by one Miguel Ruiz Herrero in the province of Guanacaste on Costa Rica's Pacific Coast.[83] The fate of the specimen is unknown. Critics agree the photo clearly shows a cougar but point out that, due to the black and white nature of the photograph, it is impossible to tell if the cougar was really black or just an unusually dark brown.

If the Herrero cougar truly was black, an amazing scientific opportunity was lost when the carcass was discarded. Was this the *cougar noire?* We will likely never know.

I was made aware of a photo, allegedly taken by trail camera in east Texas in December of 2007,

A very dark puma shot by Miguel Ruiz Herrero along the Pacific Coast of Costa Rica in 1959.

depicting an unusually dark cougar. The photo features what is undeniably a puma stalking a buck at a deer feeder. I had some reservations as to whether or not the photo was actually taken in east Texas, so I contacted well-known Texas outdoorsman Jeff Stewart who, while presenting at a conference in 2015, said that an acquaintance of his claimed to have obtained the photo on his game camera in Nacogdoches County. Mr. Stewart told me that he personally downloaded the image from the SD card, just as he stated at a 2015 conference,[84] but could not definitively say where the photo was taken. If, indeed, the photo was snapped in Texas, it is especially compelling to me, but what is seen in the photo is much more important than where it was taken. The cougar in the photo is very dark. It is not a stretch to think that someone catching a glimpse of this cat might mistake it for being black. The question is, if cougars can get this dark, can they get darker still, or even solid black?

A trail camera photo, allegedly captured in Nacogdoches County, Texas, showing a standoff between a buck and a very dark puma.
(Jeff Stewart)

Of more recent vintage is a series of reports made by citizens of northwest Waco of a family of four "black mountain lions" in March of 2013.[85] Several witnesses came forward during the flap of sightings. Some people claimed to have seen all four cats at one time – described as a mother and three young cubs – while others saw only one or two at a time. The one thing all witnesses agreed upon is that these cats had long tails and were black. The sizes of the cats seen, according to those who reported sightings, ranged from German shepherd-sized to collie-sized. One witness added that the adults were as tall at the shoulder as the rear bumper of her 2006 Ford Mustang.

Several pets in the neighborhood were killed or seriously injured by the roving wild cats. Some of the injured animals were taken to the Northside Animal Hospital on MacArthur Drive where veterinarian Dr. Jerry Stewart confirmed that whatever attacked the pets, was not "domesticated."[86] Cora Bickly of China Spring described the cat she saw as big and black, with lime green eyes and a long tail.[87]

Animal control officers took the sightings seriously enough to deploy multiple traps in an effort to capture whatever wild animal might be responsible for the sightings and pet deaths. While trapping proved to be unsuccessful, an animal control officer was able to view large paw prints left on the sliding glass patio door of a woman known only as Sarah. "The animal control officer put his hand up next to the paw print on the glass door and it was almost as big as his hand," said Sarah's daughter, Julie. "He said, 'That is one big kitty.'" Also of interest in this case were the comments of Jim Fleshman of Waco's Cameron Park Zoo who is reported to have said that, "While most mountain lions have brown fur, it is possible that there are those with a color mutation known as black melanistic."[88] If accurately quoted, this statement is outside the norm of what most big cat experts believe about the coloration of cougars.

There are obviously problems with the melanistic cougar theory. Most witnesses who claim to have seen a black panther describe a solid black cat. Occasionally, an individual describes seeing spots or markings on the coat when the light hit it just right, but I have never heard of or seen a modern report where the cat in question was described as anything but a solid black. Even if cougars can be black – a dicey assumption to be sure – they are likely not going to be monochromatic. If the descriptions given by de Buffon, Pennant, and others of the *cougar noire* are accurate – and there is no reason to believe they are not – the specimens exhibited lighter coloring on their ventral surfaces. Likewise, the account of William Thomson describes a cougar that is black dorsally but a much lighter grey on the throat, chest, and belly.

While it cannot be determined with 100% certainty that the cougar in the Herrero photo is black and not just a very dark brown, what can be seen is that the cat is much lighter in color on its underside. Admittedly, the belly and throat of the cougar in the east Texas photo are harder to see, but what can be seen on the cat is a muzzle much lighter in color than what is visible on the rest of the body. This characteristic of being dark on top and light underneath simply does not jibe well with the description given by most people who claim to have seen a black panther. That being the case, to simply assume that melanistic cougars are the answer to the black panther mystery would likely be a mistake.

It is a virtual certainty that, on occasion, cougars have been mistaken for black panthers. There could be many reasons for this. Low light conditions, unusually dark brown individuals, or even an animal with a wet coat could all be mistaken for something else if the sighting is fleeting. The fact that the cougar's size is a match for what many black panther witnesses report – and the aforementioned circumstances, which could lead to the misidentification of this cat – provide more than enough justification to keep the mountain lion high on our list of suspects in this black panther mystery.

Can cougar sightings adequately explain all sightings? No, but I do believe we have added another piece to the black panther puzzle.

8

The Suspects: Jaguarundi

SIGHTINGS OF MELANISTIC JAGUARS AND COUGARS under low-light conditions might account for some of the black panther encounters reported by Texans over the years but do not satisfactorily explain them all. Jaguars, if they still exist at all in the Lone Star State, are incredibly rare. Cougars are stealth in the flesh and are rarely seen during the day even in habitats with healthy breeding populations. To catch a glimpse of a mountain lion in low light conditions or at night is even more rare. There would seem to be something missing: a third suspect. Is there another wildcat in Texas that could be mistaken for the black panther of legend? Quite possibly, yes.

A jaguarundi exhibiting the dark morph could, if seen fleetingly, be mistaken for a much larger cat. (Wrangel\Dreamstime.com)

The jaguarundi (*Puma yagouaroundi*) is an odd looking, otter-like cat that is found predominantly in Mexico, Central America, and South America, but also ranges as far north as southern Texas and Arizona.[89] These wildcats are much more flexible than other New World cats when it comes to the types of habitats in which they can survive. Jaguarundis can be found in grasslands and savannas, scrubland and dense chaparral, tropical jungles, deciduous forests, swamps, and marshes.[90] While they seem to prefer primary habitats, they are able to thrive in secondary habitats as well and range from bottomlands up to elevations of about 10,000 feet. The species has also apparently learned to survive in close proximity to villages, as multiple accounts exist regarding jaguarundis living in forested areas that abut human habitation zones.[91]

Certainly, many of the habitats in which these wild cats live can be found in Texas. Chaparral and scrubland? Check. Deciduous forests and bottomlands? Check. Marshes and swamps? Again, check. Clearly, there is suitable habitat in which jaguarundis could live in the Lone Star State. If the species is present, they are going to be much easier for the general public to see than other cats, as these felids are diurnal and are most active around mid-morning. This could account for at least some sighting reports.

There are other reasons the jaguarundi needs to be considered as a possible suspect in the black panther mystery, not the least of which are its size and color. While the typical jaguarundi is only slightly larger than most domestic felids, the oddly elongated body of the cat can easily give the impression that it is much bigger. The average jaguarundi will measure anywhere from 21-30 inches from head to rump. An extremely long tail, usually about half the length of the body, can measure from 12-24 inches long. While not a heavy animal (the upper range on weight for these cats is approximately 25 lbs.), the jaguarundi is uniquely built and long-bodied. Perspective is something that is always difficult to nail down when it comes to sighting reports, and probably the most inaccurate detail related to investigators is the estimated distance between a witness and an animal during an encounter. The overall effect of the jaguarundi's elongated body, long tail, and unusual build could fool a witness who is seeing a specimen at relatively close quarters into thinking they are seeing a much larger cat at a greater distance.

The coloration and coat of the jaguarundi would seem to make it a prime candidate for misidentification as well. Unlike other small New World cats, the jaguarundi is not spotted. Jaguarundis exhibit two color morphs: a dark morph, usually a uniform black, dark brown, or charcoal grey, and a red morph that actually ranges from a honey-colored tawny to chestnut red.[92] Often, the dark morph is more common in darker, heavily forested habitats, while the lighter morph is seen more in drier scrubby areas. This is not universal, however, as both morphs have been documented in both environments.

A black or very dark brown jaguarundi could easily be mistaken for a black panther, especially if the sighting is fleeting in nature. The dark color and unmistakable long tail, along with the lack of familiarity of the general public with the species, could all combine to create a case of misidentification. Most witnesses who report black panther sightings are extremely confident what they saw was a cat and not a large canid of some kind. If a witness is unaware that this species exists, he/she will be left searching for a label to put on his/her sighting. In Texas and across the American South, the label that is most often going to be attached to a large black or very dark, long-tailed cat is going to be that of the black panther.

Over the years, I have received many sighting reports from people who claim to have seen one of these enigmatic black panthers of legend. There are quite a few cases where, due to the descriptions of size, color, and/or behavior of the animal reported by the witness, it is a distinct possibility a jaguarundi was the animal actually seen. Here are several examples of reports that fall into this category and have been published on the *Texas Cryptid Hunter* website. Other than removing the surnames of the witnesses in order to protect their privacy, the sighting reports are presented here exactly as they were submitted.

    10/1/13
    I'm not sure if this is the right place to post a sighting, but this is what I saw… On September 26, 2013, approx. 6:00

p.m., I was almost at a complete stop in my truck as I was going to turn into my property in Bishop, Texas, I noticed something dark moving slowly in the field right across from my location. The field is used to grow corn and cotton (but it has been cleaned for a while now).

The large black panther looking animal, approx. 3 1/2 feet long and about 18" in height, continued to walk across the street, right in front of me while I was in my truck, and he came into my property. I say he because the face was very masculine with a flat box top of head, it was not curved from ear to ear, his head was flat, the ears were short/little and pointy, his fur was full/thick, and tail was long and thick from end to end as the width was too. He was black, black, no spots or dark brown. He did not resemble a bobcat. He looked in my direction as he crossed in front of my truck and it appeared his eyes were light in color.

I have 2 dogs, 1 Great Pyrenees and a 1 Catahoula. They were barking and running from one end of the 5 acres I have to the other. The next morning, I had a hen missing and feathers were scattered. What exactly is [it that] I saw??— Monika

3/5/14

I was walking with my two German shepherds out in my back pasture one morning about 7:00 in January of this year [2014], when my male shepherd came to a quick stop and stood watching something about 50 yards ahead of us. When I looked up I saw a dark colored cat about 30 pounds or so, leap about 10 feet up into a tree covered with thick brush and was gone, it had a long tail. This was off FM 414 in Cleburne, TX. Not sure what it was but a neighbor up the road said his wife had a picture that she had taken earlier. — Anonymous

7/13/14

I live in Allen, Texas and saw a large cat hunting the rabbits in our neighborhood tonight. It appeared to be about 25 lbs., maybe 2.5 to 3 feet in length with a long tail. My mom has a Maine Coon and it was significantly bigger. It looked yellow-reddish. I didn't see any spots but unsure as it was dark and I didn't want to get close. Any ideas? — Anonymous

7/8/14
My husband and I live in Lewisville TX, in an apartment complex close to the lake. There is a small field in front of our windows. When my husband was leaving for work this morning around 7:00 a.m. he got into his car and saw a large cat jump up in front of him. It jumped a few times as if it were trying to get a rabbit or something. He saw it very up close and said it was medium-dark brown in color, looked to be about 3 feet long or longer with a long tail, large hind leg and paws. I came out onto our balcony to see if I could spot it and I eventually did. It was in the tall grass that comes up pretty tall and you can clearly see it is up above that. — Jessica

4/22/14
I live in Fort Bend County near Katy close by West Park & Hwy 99. We have a large open field/wetland by our neighborhood. Me and my two young daughters were riding our bikes on the trails. We spotted a large cat like creature about 80 to 100 yards in front of us. It was all grey about 2 1/2' tall and about 3 1/2' to 4' long. The ears were small but stood straight up. I was unable to make out the tail. I looked up a few pics on wild cats native to southeast Texas and found a pic of a jaguarundi. It looked exactly like this from the distance we were at. — Jake

12/22/15
I live near Danbury, TX near a bayou, while on my tractor recently I thought I saw a black Labrador retriever, but when it moved I thought it was a river otter which I've seen on occasion. The animal crossed in front of me and was

> definitely a large cat with a long tail, now I know it was a jaguarundi. I have talked with several old timers here and many have seen them as kids and called them simply the big black cats with long tails. Several lived near Liverpool, TX and spotted the cats near rice fields. Hopefully they are making a comeback. — Anonymous

> 12/2/15
> About 5 years ago, maybe 2010-11, I saw medium size black cat that looked like small panther run up from the east Bosque riverback. The cat was chasing a bird that was flying just few feet above the ground. The cat ran across my lane of traffic on Lakeshore Dr. (Waco, TX). The cat was a very dark black color, about 2.5' to 3' long, guess about 25 to 35 lbs., long black tail. The cat's head was rounded shape about size of typical cantaloupe. Later saw picture of a jaguarundi cat on internet, the cat looked like that species. I've also heard what sounds like a woman screaming at night. We have a lot of wildlife in this area so I'm not sure if the numerous goat deaths are from that cat or coyotes. And I'm not sure if I've seen the same cat several times or if it was more than one cat. It looks like the photos I've seen of the jaguarundi. — Anonymous

While the range of the jaguarundi is generally thought to include extreme southern Texas and Arizona, anecdotal evidence like these reports suggests these resilient cats wander farther north and east than that, sometimes much farther. As a matter of fact, several jaguarundi sighting reports from other Gulf Coast states have been reported over the years and are worthy of discussion.

Florida actually has quite a long history with the jaguarundi. Fossils found along the Ichetucknee River in Columbia County and Rock Springs in Orange County appear to be jaguarundi remains, though this is in dispute. The similarity in size and shape of the alleged jaguarundi fossils in question make them nearly impossible to distinguish from those of a margay (*Leopardus wiedii*), which has led to the controversy.[93] Other fossil finds in Brevard and Marion counties suggest this cat was present in Florida during the last ice age. What is unclear is whether or not the jaguarundi survived from prehistoric times to the present. Not surprisingly, opinions are all over the board, with some scientists believing the cat died out or retreated to its former range when the ice age ended, and some concluding the cat has survived, albeit in small numbers, into modern times.

There is another scenario that could explain the seemingly aberrant population of jaguarundi in Florida: human introduction. This is by far the most accepted theory as to how the species might have come to live in the Sunshine State. The theory most often credits (blames?) an unknown writer who lived near Chiefland for releasing jaguarundis in remote locales ranging from state parks to wildlife refuges. The mysterious writer allegedly had ties to Central America and visited the region often. Why this writer would obtain jaguarundi specimens only to release them in Florida is unknown, but the theory gained considerable traction when noted herpetologist and wildlife expert Wilfred T. Neill mentioned this scenario in some of his writings.[94]

With a bit more digging, the theory becomes even more plausible. It seems there was an author by the name of A. Hyatt Verrill who specialized in books about the Aztecs and Mayans of Mexico and Central America who made Chiefland his home in the 1940s.[95] Did Verrill import jaguarundis only to release them into the wilds of Florida? We will likely never know. What we do know, however, is that people are seeing otter-like cats matching the description of the jaguarundi in Florida. Reports have become so common that several groups have organized and placed camera traps in the wilderness in an effort to get a photo of this elusive cat.

The gap between the eastern border of Texas and the western edge of the Florida panhandle is large: approximately 420 miles. Are there any reports of jaguarundi anywhere in between? Indeed, there are. In November of 2014, a reader submitted to me a photo depicting a large black cat moving away from the camera through a heavily forested area. According to the reader, the photo was taken by a game camera in the woods of Alabama. The subject is quite obviously a cat of some kind. No one would dispute that. Too, at least from the perspective we have, it would appear to be larger than what would normally be seen in a domestic/feral. The cat appears robust and thick but not terribly tall at the shoulder. The characteristic long tail, with the thick, rounded tip so often reported by people claiming to have seen black panthers, is clearly visible. The animal is black. It is not a trick of light or a case where the animal is in shadow giving the illusion of melanism or a dark morph. From what I can tell – and I will be the first to admit that I am no expert photo analyst – the photo appears genuine. In addition, the terrain looks very much like the forested areas that run from east Texas across the South. The picture certainly looks like it could have been taken in the woods of Alabama.

This photo was sent in by a Texas Cryptid Hunter *reader and was allegedly taken via trail camera in the woods of Alabama.*
(Texas Cryptid Hunter)

There are, however, several reasons the Alabama photo cannot be deemed truly solid evidence. First, my requests for additional details from the reader went unanswered. Second, some of the hallmarks usually found on a picture taken by a game camera are notably absent on the photo: there is no time stamp, date, or company logo in the photo. If it is a game camera photo, it has been cropped. There are numerous reasons a person might want to crop such a photo before sending it in for publication on a blog or website, not the least of which would be if his name or the camera location appeared on it, but we must keep in mind that the photo has been altered to some degree.

As is often the case, scale is also an issue. The cat in the photo certainly looks to be larger than a domestic/feral, but we know nothing regarding how high the camera was mounted, the angle at which it was set, etc. These are factors that can truly affect what we are seeing. For example, the tree to the right of the cat appears to be pretty large in diameter in the photo. The impression one gets is that the cat is walking right by it. That is not quite the case though, as the tree to the right is actually in the foreground and closer to the camera than the cat. If the cat were right next to the tree, we would be seeing the spot where the tree meets the ground. We cannot see that in this image; therefore, the tree must be in the foreground. The subject has already walked by the tree and is now well past it. How far past? It is hard to say. If the cat is just a step or two past the tree, then it would seem the animal is pretty big. If the cat is five or six feet past the tree, then maybe it is not that large at all. That being the case, we cannot really make a definitive call on the size of the animal.

Still, it is one of the more intriguing black panther photos I have examined. It may very well be a photo of a jaguarundi.

I was recently made aware of another interesting jaguarundi event in Alabama back in the mid 1970s. A reader sent me a clipping from the January 25, 1975, edition of the *Mobile Register* detailing the capture of a jaguarundi outside of Birmingham by a man named J.N. Biddy. According to the article, Mr. Biddy heard his three dogs baying and went to investigate. What he found upon arriving at the scene was a small, cat-like, reddish-brown animal with a 10-inch tale, rounded ears, and unusually long body. Mr. Biddy popped the cat on the head with a stick when it hissed at him and then penned it up in an old chicken coop.

Eventually, Mr. Biddy turned the cat over to the Birmingham Zoo. Zoo director Bob Truett said, "I'll bet somebody bought him in a pet shop and turned him loose." Truett estimated the young cat was only five months old.[96] The article was accompanied by a photo of Mr. Biddy with what is unquestionably a jaguarundi. The real question here is whether this cat was an exotic pet that was released by its owner when it became too difficult to handle or if it was born in the woods of Alabama.

J.N. Biddy and the jaguarundi he captured on his property.
(Mobile Press-Register)

Another photo, sent to me in October of 2013 by a follower of the *Texas Cryptid Hunter* website, clearly shows a jaguarundi, in my opinion. According to the reader, this photo was found on a hunting forum and was allegedly taken in Mississippi. The inability to trace this photo back to its true origin is frustrating and prevents us from considering it proof that jaguarundis are living in Mississippi. I have no doubt the photo shows this species; what I cannot say absolutely for sure is where the photo was taken. Some have expressed concerns due to the fact that the jaguarundi appears in such close proximity to a deer in the photo, but I do not share that particular concern. Jaguarundis hunt smaller game, and a full-grown deer would have little to worry about from this species. Others point to the light color of the cat in the photo as a problem, but as previously mentioned jaguarundis can exhibit two different color morphs. Cats sporting the dark morph can be black, dark brown, or charcoal gray, while those exhibiting the light morph can be tawny to reddish. I feel this is simply a photo of a jaguarundi exhibiting the lighter morph. If this photo was taken in Mississippi, experts will need to reexamine some basic questions regarding the range of the species.

This photo of what appears to be a jaguarundi was allegedly snapped in Mississippi. Efforts to confirm the photo location have been unsuccessful.
(Texas Cryptid Hunter)

To sum it up, the jaguarundi is native to Texas, though current population numbers are unknown; does exhibit a black, very dark brown, and/or charcoal gray colored coat; and can be larger than most domestic/feral cats. In addition, the general public is not familiar with the species, making the likelihood of misidentification very likely. Jaguarundi sightings are not a logical explanation for all black panther sightings in Texas or the American South. Most of the reports I receive describe a cat much too large for a jaguarundi to have been the culprit. Still, this rare "otter cat" must remain on our list of suspects. I strongly suspect the jaguarundi is at least one piece in the black panther puzzle.

9

The Suspects: Giant Feral Cats

MOST PEOPLE WOULD SCOFF AT THE NOTION that a normal domestic cat (*Felis catus*), even one gone feral, could ever be mistaken for a black panther. After all, everyone knows what a house cat looks like. How could anyone mistake one of the most common pets in the Unites States for a 75-150 lb. beast? The truth is that the likelihood of just such a mistake might be greater than most realize. Most witnesses can tell you exactly where they were located when they saw a big cat; however, trying to nail down the exact spot where the animal was standing or traveling often proves to be a much more difficult proposition. A miscalculation of only a few yards can truly skew perspective and make an animal appear much larger than it really is. It is safe to assume, in some cases, that witnesses saw a cat much smaller than they reported, not realizing it was closer to them than they thought. Despite this, it is highly unlikely that a significant number of witnesses who claim to have encountered a black panther misidentified a common-sized cat. Does that mean that the feral cat should not be considered a suspect in the black panther mystery? Not necessarily.

Before going any further, it is important to understand exactly what a feral cat is and how common it is in North America. A great number of people think a feral is the same thing as a stray: someone's pet that escaped, was lost, or was dumped when it became too problematic. This would be inaccurate. A true feral is the progeny or descendent of domestic or stray cats but has grown up without any human contact.[97] They are true wild animals in every sense. Feral cats may, in many cases, live in urban environments, but they are wild animals nonetheless.

The largest cities and smallest municipalities are often equipped to deal with stray or feral dogs but, for decades, have done little or nothing to deal with the growing cat problem. For this reason, the feral cat population has exploded. It is estimated that 70 million feral cats live in the United States, and they are causing a multitude of problems.[98] For example, feral cats have been blamed for precipitous drops in bird populations across the country. These cats prey on common birds like cardinals, blue jays, robins, and wrens, but also endangered species. One such example is in California where, according to Ron Jurek, a wildlife biologist with the California Department of Fish and Game, feral cats have been blamed for decimating entire colonies of California least terns, a federally recognized endangered species that nests along the west coast. He said, "Cats do kill wildlife to a significant degree."[99]

But Jurek may have vastly understated the scale of the problem. Christopher Lever has extensively researched and written about invasive vertebrates in several books and feels feral cats are responsible for the extinction of at least 33 species of birds and various species of small mammals and reptiles around the world.[100] A 2013 study concluded that free-ranging feral cats kill 1.3-4.0 billion birds and 6.3-22.3 billion mammals every year, making them, quite likely, the greatest source of anthropogenic mortality for birds and mammals in the United States.[101]

Not everyone agrees that feral cats are having such a large impact on wildlife populations, but that is not really the point here. What is important to note, for our purposes, is that these, essentially, wild cats are present from coast to coast here in the United States in massive numbers.

Now that it has been established that there is a huge population of feral cats roaming both the rural and urban areas of our country, it must now be asked if the presence of these cats explain any of the black panther sightings in Texas and the American South. As has been noted previously, it is highly unlikely that anyone who catches more than the most fleeting of glimpses of a typical feral cat could mistake it for a panther-sized animal; therefore, the feral cannot be responsible for these sightings unless they are growing to unusually large sizes. As it turns out, some people believe that is exactly what is happening.

A look at what has been going on in Australia for decades might give us some insight into what may currently be happening in North America, Texas, and the South in particular.

Some of the most unique and dangerous wildlife on the planet is found in Australia. Great white sharks and box jellyfish lurk in the surf. Giant spiders, voracious dingoes, and some of the most dangerous and venomous snakes on the planet call the continent home. One thing the land down under has never had, however, is an indigenous species of big cat. Even so, hundreds of reports of large, black, cat-like animals have poured into the offices of Australian government and wildlife officials from the mid 1800s to the present day. The government has offered some possible explanations for the sightings, explanations that should sound very familiar to anyone who has reported a black panther sighting to wildlife officials here in the United States. Officials have posited that the animals in question are likely descendants of U.S. military mascots released into the Australian bush at the conclusion of World War II, unreported escapees from zoos or wildlife parks, misidentified large dogs, big cats that escaped from wrecked circus and animal menagerie trains during the late 1800s-early 1900s,* or ordinary feral cats. Again, the theories that have been offered up are standard fare and sound woefully familiar; but should they be dismissed?

When it comes to the feral cat theory, maybe not. According to many scientists, the most destructive animal in Australia is none other than the feral cat. It is estimated that there are 12 million such cats in Australia, descendants of domestics that were introduced here intentionally by British settlers and unintentionally via Dutch shipwrecks along the west coast of the continent in the early 1800s. The number of domestic cats exploded after 1804 as intentional releases were conducted in an effort to control other feral invaders such as rabbits, rats, and mice.[102] A mere 15 years after the misguided release of these domestic cats, there were firmly established feral populations across the entire continent.

---

* My research seems to indicate that circus trains were the single most dangerous form of transportation ever devised by man.

Australia is especially vulnerable to invasive predators as its wildlife – being isolated for millions of years – evolved to be highly specialized. All indigenous wildlife fits into a niche here, and when the natural balance is disturbed, entire species can go extinct in a shockingly short amount of time. Feral cats, outside of the dingo – also an introduced species – have no natural predators to keep them in check and, according to many, are wrecking the balance of things in Australia. They are free to roam wild with little or nothing to stop them from preying upon indigenous animals that have not evolved any defenses against them.[103] Wildlife mortality estimates show they are doing just that. According to numbers published by the Australian government, the approximately 12 million feral cats in the country are responsible for killing about 75 million native animals daily and are believed to be at least partially responsible for the extinction of several species.[104]

Worse yet, there is some tantalizing evidence suggesting that Australia's feral cats might be growing to enormous sizes. On May 9, 2001, Wayne and Gail Pound were going about their usual early morning routines when Gail happened to look out of her bedroom window and saw a large feral cat in the brush. Her attention quickly shifted from the feral cat to an enormously large feline that emerged from the bush shortly thereafter. Gail was then joined by her husband, and the couple watched the unlikely felid duo for several minutes. In an interview with Australian Channel Nine's *A Current Affair* program, Gail said, "We were quite mesmerized." Wayne added, "I got the binoculars and had a good look at it and I was still looking at it and, all of a sudden, it got up and I said 'no, hang on, that's a giant cat' and Gail yelled out 'that's a leopard!' I said 'no, hang on, that's a panther!'"[105] It was at this point that the Pounds retrieved their video camera and began shooting. The video was captured in broad daylight and starts out focused on an average looking gray domestic cat. Shortly into the filming, the camera pans right in time to see a very large black cat that is easily twice the size of its grey counterpart. Some have estimated the larger cat had an overall length of 5-feet or more. Despite its huge size, it exhibits clear signs of being a domestic/feral.

This large black cat was photographed via trail camera in east Texas. It is estimated that the cat weighed in excess of 20 lbs. (Jeff Stewart)

After viewing the footage at a conference on Australian big cats, Darren Nash of *Tetrapod Zoology* described the creature – which by now had been dubbed the Lithgow panther – as having "vertical pupils, pointed ears, and a dainty snout quite unlike the deeper snout of the large cats." Nash went on to say that the shoulder blades of the black cat appeared proportionally big, and it was significantly more muscular in appearance than the ordinary grey cat. Strangely, the normal-sized cat seems to show no sign of concern at the proximity of this much larger predator that was estimated to be no more than 10-feet away. The video even impressed some highly-qualified wildlife experts. New South Wales Department of Agriculture exotic animal specialist Bill Atkinson said, "That's a very big cat – I would say, by the size of it, it could be a panther."[106]

Another sighting of what can only be described as an enormous black cat was logged by a Senior Constable Paul Semmut in August of 2004: "It was on Scenic Hill, on Chifley Road, on the eastern side of the War Memorial at about 2:00 a.m. I was driving by myself and I almost ran over the thing. It was pretty close. It was about 1-meter long and had black, silky fur. The way it ran off it looked like a cat. My first reaction was that it was a damn big cat." Senior Constable Semmut added that he had heard of reports in the area previously but had never given them much thought as they were not true law enforcement matters. "I've always been a real skeptic about these reports but now I'm a believer," he said.[107]

An interesting bit of footage from Australia was shot in late 2004 by Andrew Burstyn at Dunkeld in southern Grampians, Victoria. The footage features a black cat that looks much more like a feral than it does a leopard or puma. It features a tapered abdomen, a tail shorter than would be expected in a true big cat, and a head shape more reminiscent of domestic/feral than a puma or leopard. The Dunkeld cat, however, appears very large. The Dunkeld footage actually gives us at least an idea as to the size of the cat as it walks within a few meters of an adult kangaroo. Burstyn estimated the height of the cat's shoulder at 75 cm (29.5 inches) which would make it much larger than any common feral.[108] The footage was examined by a Melbourne Zoo official named Noel Harcourt who concluded that the animal in the video was a feral cat and not a leopard, puma, or any other non-native exotic. Harcourt did not, however, comment on the exceptionally large dimensions exhibited by the Dunkeld cat.

In 2005, a hunter named Kurt Engel shot a large black cat that was the size of a small leopard.[109] The Gippsland panther, as it has come to be called, allegedly measured between 5- and 6-feet from nose to tail. While photos of this cat do exist, none that have been released publicly provides absolute scale. Engel claims to have dumped the body in a river near his home not too long after shooting the cat. He did, however, keep the tail as a souvenir, and it has been examined by scientists. The tail alone measured more than 2-feet in length and was proven to belong to *Felis catus* through DNA testing.[110]

The Gippsland case is not without some problems. As mentioned previously, the body was discarded and the tail provided did not contain vertebrae. This makes it possible that some of the skin/fur included might have come from the back of the cat, making the tail appear longer than it was in actuality. Also, some of the photos that have been published thus far appear to show some forced perspective. Still, even taking these factors into consideration, there is little argument the Gippsland cat is unusually large.

The Gippsland panther, as it came to be known, was a feral cat of truly astounding size. (Kurt Engel)

The Australian government has exhibited some interest in these big cat reports. In response to literally decades of reports from residents of Victoria detailing livestock kills and sightings of panthers, the government commissioned a study by the Department of Sustainability and Environment (DSE) headed by zoologist Peter Menkhorst in 2002. Menkhorst and his colleagues could find no evidence that true big cats existed in Victoria. Instead, they concluded that sightings could likely be attributed to the presence of large feral cats.[111] This conclusion infuriated many who claimed to have seen big cats in Australia but, perhaps, it should not have. To a zoologist or biologist, a panther is a specific and already documented animal: a puma. To a farmer or rancher, any large black cat is going to be labeled a panther. (Semantics again?) Menkhorst is likely right to conclude that there are no panthers, i.e. pumas, living in Victoria; however, it could be that witnesses claiming to have seen large, black, puma-sized cats are also correct. What they are seeing may not be leopards or cougars, but they might be unusually large black feral cats. This begs the question, just how large is "unusually large," and why would these cats be growing to sizes that equate to that of small leopards?

Before delving into those questions, it might first be a good idea to see just how big a domestic cat can actually get. Certainly, different breeds achieve different heights, lengths, weights, etc. but from a general perspective, how big do domestic cats grow? On average, domestic cats will grow to measure no more than 85 centimeters (33.46 inches) from nose to the tip of the tail and weigh 6.4 kilograms (14.1 lbs.). Again, these are averages, meaning some breeds will measure and weigh more than these numbers while others will measure and weigh less. The largest Australian domestic cat on record was a tabby named Himmy that measured 96.5 centimeters (32.17 inches) in length and weighed in at a stout 21.3 kilograms (46.95 lbs.).[112] With this information in mind, a look at three of Australia's most well-known giant feral cats is in order:

Cat	Avg. length	Avg. weight
Average domestic cat:	85cm/33.46"	6.4kg/14.1 lbs.
Kurt Engel Cat:	170cm/66.93"	30kg/66.14 lbs.[113]
Alpine Man Cat:	123cm/48.43"	10kg/22.04 lbs.[114]
Larry Beppington Cat:	117cm/46.06"	10kg/22.04 lbs.[115]

It is plain to see from these numbers that at least some of Australia's feral cats are growing abnormally large. The Gippsland cat shot by Kurt Engel may be an outlier, but eyewitness testimony, along with measurements gleaned from specimens taken by other hunters, seems to indicate that the common moggy is quickly becoming anything but down under. Natural selection favors the biggest and the strongest; these are the animals that survive and breed. Are the over-sized ferals of Australia the progeny of the heartiest cats in the bush, or are they something else entirely? Why are these large cats almost always black? The answers remain elusive.

While the evidence that feral cats are growing to monstrous sizes in Australia is far from concrete, anecdotally, it is extremely interesting.

If feral cats are growing larger down under, there really is no reason to think they could not be doing the same here in North America. Could feral cats be growing larger to fill the predatory niche that was left vacant by the extirpation of most wolves, black bears, and cougars in Texas and the American South? It is an interesting theory to ponder. Even if North American feral cats are not growing into immense cougar-sized animals, if they are capable of growing into the 50 lb. range and measuring between 3.5-4.0 feet from nose to tail, they would have to be considered prime suspects in the black panther mystery. Certainly, most people are not prepared to see a common feral cat of such dimensions and jumping to the panther conclusion would be understandable. Are there any black panther reports where the description of the cat given by the witness fits the large feral cat theory? Absolutely. I also strongly suspect that at least some jaguarundi sightings are the result of a misidentification of an unusually large feral cat.

Photo of a large black cat taken near Lara, Australia. The head of this cat is reminiscent of a domestic/feral. (Melbourne Herald Sun)

Based on the fact that huge populations of feral cats exist in the United States; that they can survive in practically any type of environment; and the tantalizing evidence – anecdotal though it may be – that these cats can, under some conditions, grow to shockingly large sizes in Australia (a country with regions ranging from desert to thick forests, not unlike Texas), feral cats must be kept on our list of suspects in the black panther mystery. Feral cats cannot account for all sightings, but I do believe they are yet another piece to the black panther puzzle, a puzzle that is quickly beginning to take shape.

10

The Suspects: Escaped Exotics

THERE SEEM TO BE TWO COMMON RESPONSES from wildlife officials when a sighting of a black panther is reported. The most common reply to a witness is that they must be mistaken, as there is no such thing as a black panther. You must have seen a dog or a bobcat is something that is heard often. In fairness to wildlife officials, fewer and fewer people are familiar with wildlife as society becomes more and more urban. Mistakes do happen. I can personally attest to this fact as I receive photos on a regular basis from readers claiming to have photographed a mountain lion or panther. I used to get quite excited when I saw these emails, but experience has taught me to temper my enthusiasm, as almost without exception, I find myself looking at a photo of a bobcat after clicking on the attachment.

That being said, there are quite a few sightings of large black cats that have been reported by witnesses who are highly qualified when it comes to knowing their wildlife. Lifelong hunters, wildlife biologists, and state park officials have all reported sightings. These incidents often get a different response. It must have been an exotic pet that has escaped or been released by its owner is what these types of witnesses hear. Could escaped exotics be an explanation for the black panther sightings in Texas and the American South? How common is exotic cat ownership? Why would someone release a dangerous, non-native animal into the wild? These are some of the questions that will be addressed in this chapter.

The idea of a melanistic leopard or a Bengal tiger living down the road in a neighbor's backyard might seem implausible on the surface, but, in fact, this sort of thing may be more common than most people realize. The exotic pet trade has exploded in the United States over the last three decades. According to the Humane Society of the United States (HSUS), the exotic pet trade is a multi-billion-dollar industry, second only to the trafficking of drugs and weapons on the black market.[116] It is estimated that the trade of exotic wildlife generates $15 billion dollars in revenue per year in the United States alone.[117]

The reasons why a person might want to own an exotic animal vary. Some people genuinely love wildlife and desire to be close to it. Some are taken in by a cute and cuddly young animal, not realizing it will grow up to be powerful and potentially dangerous. And some equate ownership of an apex predator as a status symbol. Others are taken in by the popularity of a certain animal at a given moment in time. For example, the sales of exotic turtles spiked in the 1980s due to the popularity of the "Teenage Mutant Ninja Turtles" cartoons.[118]

Whatever the reason, far more people are involved in the buying and selling of exotic and/or dangerous wildlife than most suspect. My own father, as a youth, was taken in by the allure of owning a dangerous pet when he purchased a baby alligator at a roadside menagerie in Florida while vacationing with his family. The alligator lived briefly in the bathtub of his home before it was killed by the family dog. (Another couple of years and that scenario might have been reversed.) The exotic wildlife trade is, indeed, big business the world over.

Big cats are especially hot commodities and the crown jewels of the exotic pet trade. So much so that many believe there are now more tigers in captivity in the United States than there are in the wild.[119] Leopards, cheetahs, tigers, lions, jaguars, and pumas are especially popular, as are smaller exotic cats like servals, caracals, and bobcats, which are shockingly easy to purchase. While not cheap, a quick internet search reveals these cats to be surprisingly affordable. Prices for exotic cats range from about $900 for bobcats up to $2,500 for a lion or tiger cub. Prices are higher for hard-to-get species. Basically, the rarer the cat, the more expensive it will be to purchase. The real costs, however, lie ahead… and that is where situations arise that might tempt a big cat owner to release his/her pet.

Probably the most well publicized exotic animal issue is the problem Florida is having with invasive Burmese pythons. According to the Florida Fish and Wildlife Conservation Commission, approximately 112,000 of these constrictors have been brought into the United States since 1990.[120] These snakes can grow to be up to 26-feet in length and weigh in excess of 200 lbs. It is strongly suspected that the pythons wreaking so much havoc in Everglades National Park are former pets, released by their owners after having grown too large to handle, or the progeny of released pets.[121] This same set them free scenario has presented itself with owners of other wildlife species, some of which are potentially dangerous, such as pacu,[122] cobras,[123] tegus,[124] lionfish,[125] and Nile monitors.[126] To think that owners of big cats would not do, and have not done, the same is naïve.

What could be so distressing to big cat owners that they would knowingly and willfully release their dangerous pets? We have already touched on the fact that these cats soon outgrow the cute and cuddly stage and become powerful animals with strong predatory instincts. The precious cub that was bottle fed, played with its owner, and seemed to love its adopted family will grow into a predator that is hard-wired for survival and nothing else. When big cats are mature, they no longer feel any love or affection for their mothers and would kill her for her territory if given the opportunity.[127] No matter how nurturing a big cat owner is to his/her pet, upon maturity, that cat will likely not feel any affection or respect for him/her.[128] It is at this point that these big cats begin to pose a risk. Many owners become afraid of their cats once they are mature and no longer want them. While there are reputable zoos and sanctuaries that accept exotic big cats, a few owners, for reasons of their own, choose not to go that route and simply release their cats into the wild.

Another reason the owner of an exotic big cat might have for wanting to get rid of his/her pet is financial in nature. As mentioned previously, purchasing an exotic big cat like a leopard or tiger is surprisingly easy and affordable. What many owners do not realize is that the purchase price is only a drop in the bucket of what it will eventually cost to properly care for their cat and maintain suitable facilities for it. Cages, vehicles capable of transporting cages, permit and licensing fees (often recurring yearly), veterinary care, liability insurance, and habitat maintenance will run into the tens of thousands of dollars. All in all, a big cat owner can expect to spend upwards of $94,000 in year one and approximately $8,000, on average, per year for the life of the cat.[129] Few things make people desperate faster than falling into dire financial straits, and desperate people do desperate things in an effort to improve their situation. Releasing an expensive big cat into the wild falls under this umbrella.

While the release of exotic big cats into the wildernesses of North America has no doubt occurred, it is likely not the most common way these predators end up free. Most owners of these exotic pets do go to great lengths to find good homes for their cats. There is another way, however, that an exotic big cat might find its way into the wild, and that is by escape. This scenario is often proposed by wildlife officials in an effort to explain sightings of black panthers and one that I scoffed at for years. How could big cats just be released or escape, and no one finds out about it? After doing research for this book, I have had second thoughts about possible escaped or released pets accounting for at least some sightings.

While we live in an era of big government in which it feels like nearly every aspect of life is heavily regulated, the process of purchasing and owning exotic cats is an area that, in many states, has escaped notice or simply been ignored by legislators. Some states have no laws at all regarding the ownership of exotic big cats and leave it up to individual municipalities to decide on regulations in their jurisdiction. This leads to very little oversight, which, in turn, leads to shoddy enforcement of enclosure regulations and big cat care. Some states have very basic permit or license requirements, while others do ban private ownership of all or types of exotic wild animals.

For our purposes, we will concentrate on the 13 states collectively referred to as the American South. This basic chart provides an overview of each state's laws relating to private possession and ownership of exotic animals.

100 *Shadow Cats*

This young female tiger was found wandering the streets of Conroe, Texas in 2016. She was wearing a collar and leash when found.
(The Venture/*Erin Poole*)

States with a ban on private ownership of exotic animals – at least large cats.[130]	Georgia, Kentucky
States with a partial ban on private ownership of exotic animals – allowing ownership of some species but not others.[131]	Arkansas, Florida, Louisiana, Tennessee, Virginia
States that require the owner of exotic animals to obtain a license or permit from the relevant state agency to privately possess the animal.[132]	Mississippi, Oklahoma, Texas
States with no license/permit requirements or statutes governing exotic ownership.[133]	Alabama, South Carolina, North Carolina

Clearly, there is little to no continuity from state to state as to how exotic big cat ownership is regulated. The situation increases the odds of poor code enforcement, subpar enclosures and habitats, underqualified ownership, and unacceptable animal medical care.

Even in states that do not issue licenses or permits for the private ownership of big cats, there are often ways around the rules. Take, for example, the state of New York, which does not allow private citizens to own big cats; however, residents can work around this by saying they are going to exhibit the animal. The United States Department of Agriculture (USDA) will issue an exhibitor's license for approximately $40. The exhibitor is then subject to USDA inspections and facilities evaluations, but these usually do not take place more than once a year.[134] Even if violations are identified during these inspections, exhibitors are often given chance after chance to correct them, which keeps shoddy facilities going for long periods of time. Cathy Liss, President of the Animal Welfare Institute, said, "Enforcement typically takes too long and the fines aren't enough." She added that some USDA inspectors are excellent but simply cannot do enough to deter irresponsible ownership of exotic animals.[135]

Such scenarios make the occasional escape all but inevitable. Some of the better documented escape events that involved big cats over the last several years, according to the Born Free USA website, include:

- Conroe, Texas (3/21/16): Animal control officers recapture a tiger seen wandering around wearing a collar and leash.[136]
- Oklahoma City, Oklahoma (5/1/15): The OKC Zoo went into lockdown mode when a tiger escaped her enclosure. The tiger was later tranquilized and caught.[137]
- Spring Hill, Florida (1/3/14): A lioness escaped her enclosure at the Survival Outreach Sanctuary after she dug under the fence into open grounds. The lioness was eventually recaptured.[138]
- Montgomery, Alabama (12/9/13): Montgomery Zoo's white tiger escaped through a break in the fence of her enclosure and got into the zoo's Asian hoof stock

exhibit. The tiger was tranquilized and recaptured.[139]
- Brooksville, Florida (6/6/12): A pet mountain lion escaped its enclosure and killed a neighbor's dog. The cougar was returned to its enclosure.[140]
- Miami, Florida (8/28/10): A 500-pound Bengal tiger escaped from his pen at Jungle Island Miami.[141]
- Ingram, Texas (1/17/09): A 300-pound Bengal tiger escaped his enclosure. The tiger was tranquilized and recaptured.[142]
- Loxahatchee, Florida (8/14/2008): A lion and a tiger escaped from McCarthy's Wildlife Sanctuary after their cages were not properly secured.[143]
- Gulf Breeze, Florida (11/14/2006): Two cougars at the Zoo of Northwest Florida escaped their enclosure due to broken fencing. The cats were recaptured three hours later.[144]
- Dallas, Texas (6/15/06): A Bengal tiger escaped its enclosure due to an electrical outage and mauled a landscape worker at the Zoo Dynamics exotic animal facility.[145]
- Bridgeport, Texas (9/10/05): A 4-month-old tiger cub was found wandering in and out of traffic near an interstate exit. The tiger had escaped from the back of his possessor's pick-up truck.[146]
- Wellington, Florida (2/17/05): A 500-pound Bengal tiger escaped from the Panther Ridge Sanctuary after his caretaker neglected to latch his cage.[147]
- Cleveland and Gaston County, North Carolina (1/8/05): Two tiger cubs were found wandering along a highway on the Gaston and Cleveland County border and were captured.[148]
- Eureka Springs, Arkansas (1/7/05): A man released his pet tiger near the town of Erbie along the Buffalo River. The tiger found his way back home, trekking some 60 miles of wilderness.[149]
- Fort Polk, Louisiana (8/6/04): A 1-year-old tiger was found on the loose in an area of thick brush near the

Fort Polk military base.[150]
- Shepherdsville, Kentucky (7/23/04): A 2-year-old snow leopard escaped while being transferred between cages. The cat ran into the woods behind the owner's house. The leopard was recaptured nine days later.[151]
- Loxahatchee, Florida (7/12/04): A 600-pound Bengal tiger escaped its enclosure and was shot and killed by a wildlife officer after being on the loose for 26 hours.[152]

These incidents chronicled are only the tip of the escaped big cat iceberg. The Born Free USA site has documented 238 different escapes of exotic big (tigers, lions, leopards, etc.) and small (bobcats, caracals, ocelots, etc.) cats. I chose to highlight some of the more recent escape events and limited my scope to states in the South. Make no mistake, though, this is going on all over the country.

Having learned about the lack of regulation of exotic big cat species in much of the United States and that escapism is a real issue, we must now ask if these renegade felids could be the source of black panther reports in Texas and the American South. In order to answer the question, we must first attempt to get an idea as to how many exotic cats are out there.

Kevin Chambers of the Feline Conservation Federation was kind enough to supply me with some numbers regarding big cat ownership in the United States. These numbers are part of the group's 2016 Wild Feline Census. The census covers exotic cat ownership in all 50 states, but for our purposes only the numbers for the 13 states generally considered to be part of the American South will be shared. Based on the numbers supplied by Mr. Chambers, this chart shows the total number of exotic cats registered in each state. I have also listed the specific number of cougars, jaguars, and leopards found in each state. It should be noted that jaguarundis were not accounted for in the census.

Feline Conservation Federation
2016 Wild Feline Census[153]

State	Total Cats	Cougars	Jaguars	Leopards
Alabama	79	9	4	4
Arkansas	133	20	3	6
Florida	853	133	21	69
Georgia	81	24	0	3
Kentucky	11	1	2	0
Louisiana	40	5	6	5
Mississippi	26	6	0	2
N. Carolina	100	19	0	2
Oklahoma	208	9	9	8
S. Carolina	107	5	2	12
Tennessee	227	19	3	9
Texas	399	49	22	12
Virginia	99	5	0	2
Totals	**2,363**	**304**	**72**	**134**

Other than cougars, jaguars, and leopards, the 2016 Wild Feline Census also counted tigers, lions, cheetahs, snow leopards, ligers, and clouded leopards. The survey illustrates the overwhelming popularity of tigers and lions in the exotic cat trade. Of the grand total of cats in the 13 southern states, I was surprised to find only 510 of them, or 22%, were species that I feel should be considered as possible suspects in the black panther mystery. Particularly surprising to me was the low number (72) of jaguars accounted for in the census. Logic would seem to dictate that, being New World cats, they would be easier to acquire than African or Asiatic leopards; however, the census does not bear that theory out. The numbers presented here are very accurate when it comes to the quantity of big cats being held in zoos, sanctuaries, rescue, and rehabilitation facilities. These facilities would all be USDA licensed and subject to government regulations and inspections. What we cannot know is how many illegally obtained cats are out there in the hands of unlicensed individuals.

While I believe the narrative that there could be a tiger or leopard in your neighbor's backyard is a bit overblown, to say that it is not happening to some degree is untrue. How likely is it, though, that released or escaped individuals are responsible for the black panther sightings in Texas and the southern United States? In my opinion (despite the evidence suggesting escapes and releases are not as unusual as many think), not very likely at all. Why? Because almost all big cats bought and sold have been in captivity their entire lives. They are totally dependent on people and have never learned the art of hunting. Many of these cats have been declawed as well, which would further hinder any efforts at taking game. These dependent cats typically do not go far or remain gone too long, as they are unable to take care of themselves. The previously cited example of the man from Eureka Springs, Arkansas, who released his pet tiger into the woods only to have it travel 60 miles and show up back on his doorstep drives home this point. Most of these released or escaped animals are recaptured or killed within a very short amount of time.

It is possible that some released or escaped melanistic leopards or jaguars have resisted the temptation to return to their human caretakers and eluded capture, and such cats could be behind some black panther visuals. However, there are several reasons I do not feel this scenario can explain all, or even most, sightings. First, the sightings of these enigmatic cats have been going on since long before the exotic pet trade came to the fore. In this book alone we have examined sightings going back as far as the 1800s, and the legends of the indigenous peoples of North America go back even farther than that. Released or escaped pets cannot explain these historical accounts. Second, while an escaped cat might explain sightings in a given area over a certain time period, it cannot possibly explain all of the sightings that have taken place from coast to coast. An escaped or released pet, even if it avoids recapture, likely will not live long. The idea that multiple escapees have, somehow, found each other in the wilderness and reproduced to the point that a breeding population of melanistic cats resulted seems extremely far-fetched. Third, as the Feline Conservation Federation's 2016 Wild Feline Census shows, tigers and lions are the most sought after species in the exotic big cat trade. There simply are not enough leopards and jaguars in captivity – even considering the possibility of a fair number of unaccounted for specimens – to logically think that released or escaped members of these species could possibly account for the hundreds of sightings across the South. Finally, I am aware of only a single incident where an exotic cat of any kind was located then recaptured or killed in an area where no escapes had been reported. That incident took place in Charlestown, Indiana, in June of 2013 when a man, who was responding to his girlfriend's complaint that a bobcat had been prowling about the property and snatching her cats, shot and killed a leopard (spotted coat).[154] The Indiana Department of Natural Resources confirmed the identity of the big cat and speculated it was an escaped pet. While there was a wildlife refuge located nearby, all of its big cats were accounted for. Not once, at least to my knowledge, has a similar circumstance with a melanistic cat occurred.

Officials feel the cat killed in Charleston, Indiana, was likely an escaped pet, but no one seems to know where it came from. Leopards like this one remain popular in the exotics trade. (Chandrava Sinha/Wikipedia Commons)

Some might not buy the explanation that the Indiana leopard was an escaped pet, but instead point to it as proof that these big cats are roaming free in the United States. Maybe, but the fact of the matter is that incidents of this kind have proven to be so rare as to be statistically irrelevant. Though not as uncommon as I once believed them to be, if escapes involving unrecovered cats were taking place on a regular basis we would be seeing reports similar to the Indiana incident much more often.

Could released or escaped melanistic jaguars or leopards be responsible for at least some black panther reports in Texas and the southern United States? I suppose so, yes; however, they simply cannot be the one and only explanation for these sightings. Personally, I do not believe escaped cats to be a significant factor in the black panther phenomenon at all. While released and/or escaped pets might be a piece of the overall puzzle, it is a very small piece, indeed.

11

The Science Behind Melanism

AT THIS POINT, we have discussed several possible suspects in the black panther mystery and why they are, or in some cases are not, the likely suspects responsible for the sightings of very large, black, long-tailed cats in Texas and the American South. Within these discussions, the term melanism has been mentioned multiple times. I feel it is important to be clear on exactly what this term means so, at this point, I would like to pause and dig into the science behind what causes individuals within some species to display melanism on occasion, while individuals of other species do not. To truly understand what is going on when it comes to melanism, it is necessary to delve into the science of genetics. Some reading this may not be interested in the science behind melanism and that is okay. After all, you do not have to understand the inner working of an internal combustion engine to enjoy driving a car. But I feel that if we are to fully understand what is going on regarding the black panther phenomenon, at least a cursory review of the science behind melanism is in order.

Genetics, though fascinating, is an extremely complex science, and there is simply no way to explain all the factors at play here in the space we have. That being the case, I will not attempt to wade into those deep waters. Instead, what I hope to do in this chapter is simply touch on the basics of why some cats are black and some are not.

Before getting started, I feel it would be beneficial to identify some terms and their definitions which will be used in this chapter. Understanding what these terms mean is crucial to understanding the concepts that are going to be discussed. The list of terms in this table is not all-

The Science Behind Melanism 109

inclusive, but I feel confident that what is not defined here are terms that will be familiar to most people who have survived high school biology.

Agouti: The name given to the genes that control hair color patterns.[155]

Allele: One of a series of alternative forms of a given gene, differing in DNA sequence, and affecting the functioning of a single product (RNA and/or protein).[156]

Chromosome: Linear or circular strands of DNA that contain genes.[157]

Dominant/Dominance: Referring to alleles that fully manifest their phenotype when present in the heterozygous state.[158]

Frequency: The number of times some event occurs within a group of individuals.[159]

Gene: A hereditary unit that occupies a specific position (locus) within the genome and has one or more specific effects upon the phenotype of the organism.[160]

Genotype: The genetic makeup of an individual. The allele(s) possessed at a given locus.[161]

Heterozygous: A term used to describe an individual that has inherited two different alleles at one or more loci and, therefore, does not breed true.[162]

Homozygous: A term used to describe an individual that has two identical alleles at one or more loci and, therefore, breeds true.[163]

Locus: The specific location that a gene occupies in a chromosome.[164]

Melanin: A dark brown to black pigment responsible for the coloration of skin, hair, and the pigmented coat of the retina.[165]

Melanism: The hereditary production of increased melanin resulting in darker coloring.[166]

Mutation: The process by which a gene undergoes a structural change. By extension, the modified gene created and the individual manifesting the mutation.[167]

Phenotype: The observable properties of an individual.[168]

Rate: The number of mutations that occur during cell division, or the number of mutations per gamete, or per generation.[169]

Recessive: An allele or phenotype exhibited only by homozygotes.[170]

Now, back to the topic at hand. We have established that science does not recognize the black panther as an individual species. The cats described as black panthers by witnesses are almost universally assumed to be leopards or jaguars exhibiting melanism. Melanism is caused by a mutation of the Agouti signaling protein (ASIP) or the Melanocortin 1 receptor (MC1R).[171] If that sounds complicated, that is for a good reason. Not to worry, though, as all we really need to understand is that both jaguars and leopards, as well as several other species of felids, carry the genetic traits necessary to produce melanistic offspring. The mountain lion, on the other hand, does not appear to carry the genetic variant necessary to produce melanistic offspring, which explains the belief that there is no such thing as a black cougar.

For most, the term mutation has a negative connotation. While it is true that birth defects, cancer, and other diseases are often the result of genetic mutations, sometimes mutation is a good thing. Mutation is responsible for all phenotypic variation. Different eye and hair colors, the massive variety of flowers, the many types of dog breeds, etc. are all the result of mutations. Mutations occur all the time and add variety and diversity to our world. There are two basic types of mutations: somatic mutations and germ cell mutations. Somatic mutations occur in body cells that do not make eggs or sperm; therefore, they affect only the individual with the mutation. The mutation is not heritable and cannot be passed from parent to offspring.[172] Germ cell mutations occur in the sex cells that lead to embryo formation. They are different from somatic mutations in that the individual (parent) with the mutation is often unaffected. Instead, only the offspring of the individual with the mutation is affected, and the trait is heritable from that point on.[173] Melanism is a germ cell mutation, as it is something that is heritable and passed down from generation to generation.

The next logical question is: what causes mutations in the first place? The answer is complex and multi-faceted. Entire books are dedicated to this very question. The watered-down answer to the question is that mutations are usually caused by either exposure to outside agents or simply occur at random due to an error during DNA replication.[174] Mutations caused by outside agents like radiation, chemical pollution, etc. are almost always deleterious to the affected individual and species. Random, or spontaneous, mutations are not always bad.

The fact of the matter is that helpful adaptations are exhibited all over the natural world. Examples of adaptations that originated in spontaneous mutations include the white coat of the polar bear (*Ursus maritimus*), which helps it blend in to its arctic environment; the extra-large ears of the Saharan fennec fox (*Vulpes zerda*), which aids it in heat dissipation; and the coloration of the copperhead snake (*Agkistrodon contortrix*), which allows it to blend in perfectly with the leaf litter of the forests. The mutations were helpful, thus, through the process of natural selection, they were passed on to subsequent generations.

Some mutations are considered neutral, due to the fact that there is no obvious change in the physical characteristics or behaviors of a species after they occur. If, however, a mutation results in a new protein that causes a change in the function of a gene, a new phenotype can result. In other words, the mutation is observable on a macro level. When this modified gene, or allele, creates a noticeable effect, it is considered dominant over the original allele.[175]

To narrow the subject down to melanistic black cats, it is likely safe to assume that:

> – a mutation in the agouti gene occurred spontaneously in the felid species that exhibit melanism at some point in the past (some research suggests this occurred up to five times);[176]

> – the mutation created a functional change to the genes in question that led to the creation of new alleles and, by extension, new phenotypes;

> – and the original mutation was somehow advantageous to the species, or at least not deleterious, as it has not been eliminated by natural selection and continues to be passed on to offspring.

If all of this is true, then there should be some rhyme or reason to where melanistic individuals are most prevalent. These shadow cats should be located in places where their dark coats would be advantageous or, at least, not hinder their chances of survival. In the case of the leopard, that certainly appears to be the case.

In the Malaysian Peninsula, melanism in leopards approaches fixation.[177] An article published in the July 13, 2010, issue of the *Journal of Zoology* bolsters this claim. Researchers placed camera traps in 22 locations in Peninsular Malaysia and southern Thailand between 1996 and 2009. Altogether, during the 42,565 "trap nights," 445 photos of melanistic leopards were captured, while only 29 pictures of spotted leopards were taken.[178] That equates to a melanism rate of 94% in the region. All 29 of the spotted leopard photos came from cameras set up north of the Isthmus of Kra. Why would this adaptation take hold so strongly in this area while black leopards in Africa are so rarely seen? The answer is, once again, natural selection. The forests of southeast Asia are dense and dark. A black cat here would likely suffer no ill effects from its coat and, in fact, might have an advantage over its spotted relatives. Certainly, there are dark jungles in Africa, too, but leopards there spend a lot of time on savannahs and grasslands as well; a mottled coat would be of much greater use to a predator in this environment. A melanistic leopard trying to hide in the yellowed grasses of the Serengeti plains, for example, would stick out like a sore thumb, and natural selection would quickly weed out most of these dark-colored cats.

Anecdotally, this seems to be the pattern with New World jaguars, too, as it has long been rumored that more black specimens are seen in the deepest jungles of Amazonia and Central America than farther north into the more arid climes of Mexico and the American Southwest. The indigenous peoples of Central and South America have made the same claim regarding the most likely places to see dark morph jaguarundis.

Some have theorized that the black panthers seen so often in Texas and the American South are a remnant population of jaguars in which the trait of melanism has become all but fixed, as it has in the leopard population of the Malaysian Peninsula. Why the black coat would have become favored by natural selection in a North American big cat is something that can be debated, but if a population of mostly melanistic jaguars became somehow cut off from other jaguar populations that exhibit the more common rosettes, it could result in an almost totally black-coated population.

There is a way to mathematically determine the probability that a mating pair of big cats will produce melanistic offspring. During sexual reproduction, a parent is equally likely to pass on to its offspring either of the two alleles it has at each genetic locus.[179] This makes it possible to estimate the probability of specific genotypes being produced from the pairing of two individuals. For example, given two alleles from each parent, four allele combinations are possible. These combinations and their probabilities can be calculated using a Punnett square. To set up a single locus Punnett square, the genotype of each parent (alleles) is placed on the top and left side of a six-box graph. The alleles on the edges determine how the middle squares are filled in.

Once complete, a Punnett square shows the genotypes possible from crossing two individuals. Each of the four boxes in a square contains one of the four combinations of alleles possible (genotypes). The genotype in each box has a 25% probability of occurring every time the two individuals are crossed. If two boxes contain the same genotype, the probability of that genotype occurring goes up to 50%.[180] Punnett squares can be used to examine genotype probabilities from more than one locus at a time, but the resulting chart can be complex and difficult to interpret. For our purposes, we will calculate only the genotype from one locus, the alleles that determine coat coloration.

In jaguars, the allele for melanism is dominant[181] and will override a recessive allele when heterozygous pairings occur and fully manifest the black phenotype. In the Punnett squares diagrammed on the next several pages, you can see the expected distribution of coat colors from the different possible combinations of mating pairs of jaguars and how this dominant allele asserts itself in the natural world. In these diagrams, the dominant allele for melanism is represented by (A) while the recessive allele for the more common golden/tawny coat is represented by (a).

Two Homozygous (AA) Parents

	A	A
A	AA	AA
A	AA	AA

Results: 100% homozygous (AA) - melanistic

This pairing would result in 100% of the offspring being black, as only the dominant allele for melanism (A) is present. There is simply no other possibility as the recessive allele (a) for a golden/tawny coat is completely absent from the genotype.

One Heterozygous (Aa) Parent / One Homozygous (AA) Parent

	A	A
A	AA	AA
a	Aa	Aa

Results: 50% homozygous (AA) - melanistic
50% heterozygous (Aa) - melanistic

This pairing would result in 100% of the offspring having black coats as the dominant (A) allele would suppress the recessive (a) allele. It should be noted that there is a 50% chance the offspring would be homozygous for the dominant (A) allele, and a 50% chance the offspring would be heterozygous and carry one dominant allele and one recessive allele, which would factor into the color of future generations.

One Homozygous (AA) Parent / One Homozygous (aa) Parent

	A	A
a	Aa	Aa
a	Aa	Aa

Result: 100% heterozygous (Aa) - melanistic

This pairing would result in 100% of the offspring being black. Each of the cubs would be heterozygous and carry one dominant (A) allele and one recessive (a) allele. The dominant allele would suppress the recessive allele in offspring produced from this coupling, but the heterozygous genome in these offspring would have a bearing on the color of future generations.

Two Homozygous (aa) Parents

	a	a
a	aa	aa
a	aa	aa

Result: 100% homozygous (aa) – golden/tawny

This pairing would result in 100% of the offspring being golden/tawny with visible rosettes as only the recessive allele (a) is present. There is simply no other possibility as the dominant (A) allele for a melanistic coat is completely absent from the genotype.

One Homozygous (aa) Parent / One Heterozygous (Aa) Parent

	a	a
A	Aa	Aa
a	aa	aa

Result: 50% heterozygous (Aa) – melanistic
50% homozygous (aa) – golden/tawny

The pairing above would result in a 50% chance the offspring would inherit both the dominant (A) allele for melanism and the recessive (a) allele for a golden/tawny coat. These cubs would be black, as the dominant allele for melanism would suppress the recessive allele. But there is a 50% chance the offspring would inherit one recessive (a) allele from each parent. These cubs would be the normal golden/tawny color and have visible rosettes as the dominant (A) allele for melanism would be absent.

Two Heterozygous (Aa) Parents

	A	a
A	AA	Aa
a	Aa	aa

Result: 25% homozygous (AA) – melanistic
50% heterozygous (Aa) – melanistic
25% homozygous (aa) – golden/tawny

With this pairing, there would be a 25% chance the offspring would be homozygous with the dominant (A) allele; these cubs would be black. There is also a 25% chance the offspring would be homozygous for the recessive (a) allele; these cats would be golden/tawny with visible rosettes. There would be a 50% chance the cubs would be heterozygous and carry one dominant (A) allele and one recessive (a) allele; these cubs would be black as the dominant allele for melanism would suppress the recessive allele for a golden/tawny coat.

The Punnett square diagrams presented here cover the six different coupling possibilities that could occur in the wild with New World jaguars. It is easy to see how black jaguars could become very common if a small group of cats carrying the dominant (A) allele was cut off from the larger population. But such a scenario would only take place if the black coat was somehow advantageous to the species, otherwise the black coat would be eliminated by the process of natural selection.

Leopards are a completely different matter, as melanism is the result of a recessive allele in this species.[182] As a matter of fact, you could basically take all the Punnett square diagrams previously presented and reverse the outcomes to figure the probability of a leopard having melanistic offspring, but I will save you the time and trouble. All you really need to know is that only couplings that result in the offspring receiving a recessive (a) allele from each parent will produce melanistic cubs. That being the case, only a coupling between one homozygous (aa) parent and one heterozygous (Aa) parent, a coupling between two heterozygous (Aa) parents, and a coupling between two homozygous (aa) parents even have a chance to produce melanistic offspring. The scenario where one homozygous (aa) parent and one heterozygous (Aa) parent couple would result in a 50% chance melanistic cubs would be produced. The second scenario where two heterozygous (Aa) leopards couple would result in a 25% chance of melanistic offspring. Only the coupling of two homozygous (aa) parents would result in a 100% melanistic litter. That is it. Any other genotype would result in at least one dominant (A) allele at each locus, which as previously mentioned, in the case of leopards, is the allele responsible for the golden/tawny coat. This dominant allele would suppress the recessive (a) allele for melanism. It is this very limitation that makes the near fixation of melanism among the leopards of the Malaysian Peninsula so fascinating.

Pseudo-melanism is a topic that deserves a brief mention here as well, as it causes an atypical phenotype that could be misidentified as a black panther. Pseudo-melanism can be broken down into two types, each of which is fairly simple to understand. Both types are known to occur only in species that have spots or stripes. The first type of pseudo-melanism occurs when spots are bigger or more numerous than usual, say in the case of an ocelot, bobcat, or cheetah, and are so thick they obscure much of the normal colored coat beneath.[183] This type of pseudo-melanism has also been observed in tigers when their stripes are unusually wide and close together. This almost completely hides the golden/orange coat beneath. The second type of pseudo-melanism deals, once again, with dominant and recessive alleles. It seems that sometimes the dominant alleles are not completely dominant, and this leads to some of the normal coloration remaining on the animal in question. This is most commonly seen in jaguars and leopards. These animals are very dark in areas but still exhibit patches of their normal coloration. Again, while this is an oversimplification of the genetics involved it is enough to understand the basics of why some cats exhibit melanism while others do not. For those interested in delving deeper into the topic of pseudo-melanism, *Mystery Cats of the World* by Dr. Karl Shuker would be an excellent place to start.

Pseudo-melanism is exhibited in jaguars when the dominant allele for melanism fails to completely suppress the recessive allele for a golden/tawny coat. (Ron Singer/Wikipedia Commons)

There are many remaining questions and scenarios that could be discussed, but the topic about which I am most often asked is the possibility of hybridization among big cats. Could, for example, a jaguar carrying the dominant (A) allele mate with a mountain lion and, if so, could it produce black offspring? To be honest, I have had a hard time getting a straight answer out of the experts when it comes to this question. My understanding is that different species of cats can mate and produce offspring if the actual physical coupling is possible. Such offspring, as expected, would exhibit a mix of the physical characteristics, which would include coat color, of each parent.

Photos of hybrid big cats are very popular on the internet, and many people have seen photos of ligers (lion/tiger hybrid), tiguars (tiger/jaguar hybrid), etc. The prevailing opinion is that such couplings take place only in captivity, and that any viable offspring would almost certainly be sterile and not capable of reproducing. But there is some strong evidence that suggests hybridization does indeed, at least on occasion, take place in the wild, and that the progeny of these couplings are not always sterile.[184]

The case of the Florida panther is a good place to start the discussion of hybridization in the wild. Recent analyses of these pumas (*Felis concolor coryi*) have led to an inference of hybridization.[185] When the distribution of mtDNA variation among Florida panther individuals, individuals from seven other North American subspecies, three South American subspecies, and animals from a captive breeding population was compared, the Florida panther samples were found to represent two divergent lineages.[186] To the surprise of many, Florida panthers were found to be most closely related to South American subspecies and not subspecies found much closer to home in North America. This suggests that the rare, endemic population of Florida panthers had recently undergone introgressive hybridization.[187] The source of the South American mtDNA haplotype is thought to have come from the release of captive breeding individuals in southern Florida in the recent past – known as the Piper population[188]– as it would explain how these Sunshine State pumas had somehow managed to find mates with a South American lineage.

The discovery that Florida panthers have hybridized with a South American subspecies of mountain lion is surprising, but the cats are so closely related and so similar in size and appearance that it is hardly shocking that it could happen if the two subspecies found themselves in close proximity. Certainly, the problems the panthers of Florida have had finding suitable mates - most caused by man – could lead to a sort of desperation to propagate with whatever compatible species that might be found, and plays into the theory that hybridization takes place only when populations become dangerously small. There are, however, other examples where hybridization between species seems to have taken place minus any such stress.

Studies of the genus *Canis* have yielded several examples of phylogenetic nonconcordance that appear to be due to introgressive hybridization as well.[189] The red wolf (*Canis rufus*) is one such example. Researchers examining microsatellite loci from gray wolves (*Canis lupus*), red wolves, and coyotes (*Canis latrans*) found the red wolf to be intermediate in allele frequency between gray wolves and coyotes.[190] This finding led researchers to conclude that the red wolf originated "through the interbreeding of coyotes and gray wolves."[191] While the evidence for hybridization seems strong enough, some continue to argue that it is only the result of stress placed upon gray wolves due to manmade habitat disturbances. While this could certainly be the reason for recent hybridization and the growing population of what are commonly referred to as coydogs and/or coywolves in the South, it has been recognized that three divergent mtDNA types found in wolf populations could reflect the result of more ancient introgression and subsequent mtDNA evolution far before humans became a problem for these canids.[192]

To simplify, it appears that hybridization does take place in nature (at least occasionally), that the progeny of these unions are not always sterile, and that at times they actually become quite successful. Certainly, the current plights of the Florida panther and the red wolf have nothing to do with the ability of these two species to reproduce successfully and, had they been left to their own devices, these hybrid species would have been just fine.

Could black panthers be some sort of hybridized population of big cats that resulted from the coupling of two separate felid species? The example of the red wolf suggests that it is possible, but the list of new species that originated from the coupling of two distinct species is a short one. The chances that such a population of hybrid cats exists is, statistically speaking, zero. I have no problem entertaining the idea that some hybridization has occurred in the wild, most likely between mountain lions and jaguars, and possibly between bobcats and domestic/ferals, and that these infrequent unions could have produced offspring. These offspring could, theoretically, be responsible for some black panther sightings in North America, but there is practically no chance that any such hybrids could explain them all.

Perhaps the greatest remaining question of all is why some cats possess the genetics for melanism while others do not. Understand, this question has nothing to do with whether or not the trait actually expresses itself in a phenotype; rather, why is it not even a possibility in some felid species? After all, cats are all thought to have descended from a common ancestor. If so, did this ancient cat carry the genetic traits necessary for melanism to manifest? Also, if mutations can arise at random, is it truly impossible for this to have occurred in other cat species like the cougar? Clearly, this is exactly what occurred with leopards and jaguars at some point in the distant past. Is it possible this mutation for melanism has taken place in much more recent times in mountain lions and so is not as well established in their population as it is in those of the jaguar and leopard? Could natural selection be in the process of deciding if cougars should be, on occasion, black?

I am told by experts in the field that, while not absolutely impossible, the chance of such a scenario occurring is so infinitesimally small that it might as well be zero. Still, nature has a way of surprising us when given even half a chance, and the fact that this exact scenario has played out in at least 17 known species of wild cats in the world over time tells us that – terrifically long odds or not – it is not impossible.

There is so much more that could be discussed here, but I think we have covered what most people need to know about what melanism is and how it expresses itself in certain felid species and hybridization in the wild. Does this knowledge help us in our quest to solve the black panther mystery? I believe so, as once a basic understanding of the genetics behind melanism is achieved, we can look at our list of suspects and start to assess the probability behind each one being the prime culprit in this mystery.

12

Photographic Evidence

ONE COMMON REFRAIN I HEAR when it comes to the possible existence of large, black, long-tailed cats in North America - the American South and Texas in particular - is that there is no hard evidence. No carcass has been found, no road-killed specimens located, and no hunter has been able to bag one of these elusive cats. While it is true that no specimen has been obtained, it might be unwise to insist that there is no evidence supporting the possible existence of these cats. Anomalous hair and scat samples have been collected but remain unexamined by those most qualified to identify the species that left them behind. (I will detail some of the issues I have dealt with regarding hair samples in Chapter 14.)

Photographs, too, have been snapped and dismissed. I will be the first to admit that a photograph is not sufficient in and of itself to prove the existence of a novel species. Science demands a body; no argument there. I would argue, however, that photographs should not be ignored or dismissed outright. Too often, photos are deemed hoaxes for no other reason than there is no such thing as a black panther. This is unscientific and intellectually lazy. Each photo should be examined on its own merit, each back story explored, and each sighting location examined whenever possible.

In this chapter I will discuss some of the photographs referred to in the preceding chapters, along with some others that have been sent to me over the years. I am not an expert in photography or in how to digitally manipulate images, so I cannot vouch for the authenticity of these photos. What I can tell you is that these are the photos that I have found to be the most intriguing, and they have come from people whom I believe are telling me the truth. These photos represent some of the best evidence that there is a biological entity responsible for black panther sightings in Texas, the southern United States, and other parts of the world where no such animal is supposed to exist.

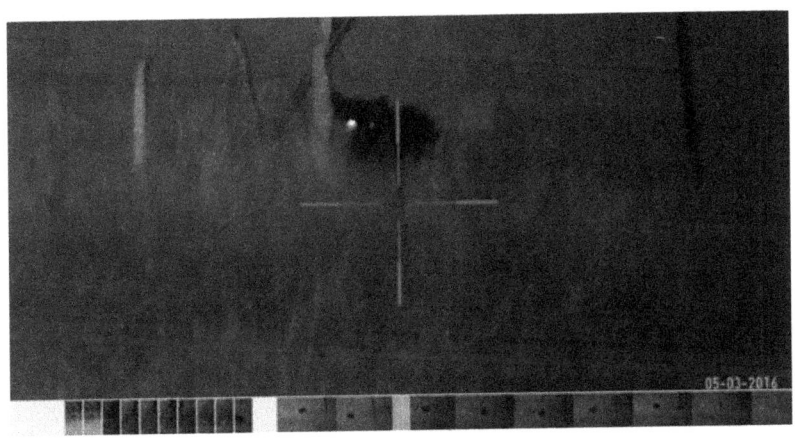

Still from a video shot by a hunter outside of Austin with an ATS night vision scope. Big cat or feral hog? (Texas Cryptid Hunter)

I received this photo via email in May of 2016. The hunter who took the video claims to have had additional pictures of the cat with a deer kill. He also said he had pictures of himself with a tape measure standing in the same location where the photos were taken that would provide scale and prove the animal was in excess of 200 lbs. The hunter told me he reported the sighting to a game warden and was told to "shoot it if you see it again." Unfortunately, my follow-up questions and requests to see the footage and additional photos went unanswered. I really do not get the impression that the animal in the photo is a hog or any other type of wildlife but cannot be certain it is a cat, either. It is interesting but inconclusive.

The cat in this photo looks to be a very large domestic/feral, in my opinion.
(Texas Cryptid Hunter)

This photo was sent to me in the early winter months of 2015. I estimate that the cat in this photo is the size of a small bobcat. The head shape, ears, and tail appear very domestic/feral to me. It is a hefty cat to be sure, and any hunter or hiker catching only a fleeting glimpse of it could be excused for jumping to the panther conclusion. Some have argued that the cat in the photo might be a jaguarundi, but I disagree with that assertion. While the angle is not perfect and the cat is not in complete profile, I just do not see the long, sinewy body shape of a jaguarundi. Neither do I see the odd-shaped and otter-like head characteristic of the species. Though I would love to be proven wrong, I strongly feel that in this photo, we are looking at a very large domestic/feral, not unlike what is being seen in Australia.

*A still shot from a video in Iberia Parish, Louisiana.
(Karen Fory)*

This photo remains one of the most convincing and intriguing black panther photos I have seen. The photo is a still from a video shot in Iberia Parish, Louisiana, on July 4, 2013, and was featured on the local news affiliate KLFY.[193] There were multiple witnesses who all claimed the cat was very large. Louisiana wildlife officials later visited the scene and, after conducting a reenactment, declared the cat had been nothing more than a domestic/feral. The family remains unconvinced of this assessment. Cathy Irwin, one of the family members present that day, said that the idea that it was a house cat just is not a possibility. "That was a dangerous animal," she said.[194] I am not much of a conspiracy guy, but I have to admit I have my doubts about the domestic/feral conclusion reached by the Louisiana wildlife officials. Everything I see in this photo and the video looks "big cat" to me. The build, the posture, head shape, tail… everything. Again, however, we can say only that the photo is intriguing but not conclusive.

The animal in this photo is quite large and appears to be a cat of some kind, but where the photo was taken is in dispute. (Daily Mail)

This photo is interesting but wrapped in controversy. The photo was brought to my attention several years ago, and I was initially quite impressed. According to the backstory I was given, the photo was snapped in 2007 in rural Lapeer County, Michigan. The controversy over where the shot was taken stems from the claims of an English couple named Herbert and Doreen Smith who state that they stumbled upon the big cat near Trowbridge, Wiltshire, in August of 2013. Mr. Smith said: "The animal was eating what we believe it had just caught. There was a lot of rabbits about so I expect it was having breakfast."[195]

An article in the *Daily Mail* documented the claims of the Smiths but did express doubt that the couple had actually taken the photo. As a matter of fact, the Lapeer County, Michigan, connection was mentioned by Shari Miller, the reporter who wrote the piece for the *Daily Mail*: "It emerged the photograph – possibly of a cougar – may have in fact been taken in Lapeer County, Michigan, in the U.S. and first published in 2007."[196]

I have included the photo here as it appears that there is more evidence suggesting the photo was taken stateside than there is supporting it having been taken in England. It is too bad the origin of the photo remains clouded, as it is a truly impressive shot, one of the best and most intriguing I have come across. In that regard, I suppose it does not really matter where it was taken, as there are not supposed to be any large, black, undocumented cats roaming the English countryside either.

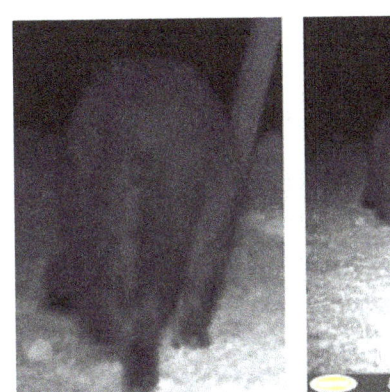

This photo was captured by a trail camera that was keeping watch over a deer feeder in the Texas Hill Country. (Texas Cryptid Hunter)

This photo is undoubtedly of a cat. The debate in this case rages around the size of the felid. The photo was taken by a trail camera watching over a feeder in the Texas Hill Country. While the quality of the photo is not great, cat-like pads are evident, as is the long thick tail so often reported. I emailed a copy of the photo to noted Texas author and naturalist Chester Moore, Jr., in order to get his opinion. He said, "The animal in the photo is definitely a cat," and "The body position and short legs point to the jaguarundi, along with the dark color."[197]

This photo was sent to me in February of 2017 and was taken near Rocky Branch, Texas. (Alex Espinoza)

This photo came to me via a follower of the *Texas Cryptid Hunter* Facebook page in February of 2017. Allegedly, the photo was taken early one foggy morning near the small rural community of Rocky Branch, Texas. While the animal in the photo is a long way from the photographer, there is little doubt as to its identity. The animal is clearly a cat. An extraordinarily long tail, similar to what so many witnesses have reported, is clearly evident. Some people with whom I've shared this photo think that it is "too perfect," and the cat might actually be some kind of cut-out. I suppose that anything is possible, but in my opinion, there is less evidence supporting a hoax than there is for the image being genuine. Thus, I include the photo here. There is simply no ambiguity with this one. It is either a very large and dark-colored cat or a flat-out fabrication. If it is real, then it is one of the better black panther photos I have seen. It should be clear by now that a photograph alone will never be enough to prove the existence of these cats. Even a really good shot like this one, or a video like the Iberia Parish footage, just does not meet the high evidentiary requirements necessary to prove these shadow cats exist.

An interesting photo snapped from a deer blind outside of Llano, Texas.
(Texas Cryptid Hunter)

This photo was taken outside of Llano, Texas, in November of 2015. The hunter who snapped the photo felt the cat was too big to be a domestic/feral. While the cat is very thick and does display the muscular hindquarters so often reported, my opinion is that it is a domestic/feral. It seems too bulky and short-bodied to be a jaguarundi and not large enough to be one of the big cats like a leopard or jaguar. Also, the head is reminiscent of a domestic/feral. I will say that it appears to be on the large side for a normal cat, but even using the young doe in the background for scale, it is difficult to tell. How far is the cat from the doe? Your guess is as good as mine. What can be discerned is that if the cat is a good deal closer to the hunter than the doe, then it is not much, if any, bigger than a normal domestic/feral. If, however, the cat is fairly close to the doe, it is unusually large for a normal cat. Whatever the case, it appears to have the full attention of that doe.

Photo taken by a trail camera in eastern Oklahoma.
(Texas Cryptid Hunter)

This shot is interesting. The photo was allegedly snapped in the foothills of the Ouachitas in eastern Oklahoma, an area with which I am very familiar. The animal in the photo is large; the feeder to the right of the animal provides enough scale to prove that. The animal has a large head and thick, muscular neck that appear very jaguar-like to me. This could be a trick of perspective or a result of the animal looking slightly to its right, but based on what we can see, it looks like a big cat. The animal also has the thick body so common in healthy and mature big cats and lacks the dog-like taper, or thinning, in the abdomen. Some have cited the appearance of the tail as a reason to doubt the animal in the photo is some kind of cat. It does appear a bit thin and short, but like the head, this could be a result of the position of the animal at the moment when the photo was taken. I find this image very compelling, but I will have to join those who consider it not definitive. Maybe it is becoming obvious why people who have seen these cats roll their eyes when asked, "If they are real, then why are there no pictures?" Clearly, there are photos, but animals rarely pose politely to have their portraits taken.

A reader of the Texas Cryptid Hunter *website submitted this photo in July of 2014. It was taken in Rowlett near Lake Ray Hubbard.*
(Texas Cryptid Hunter)

Admittedly, at first glance, this photo does not appear very impressive. It features a cat slinking along a temporary barrier near Lake Ray Hubbard northeast of Dallas, Texas. The cat is difficult to see in the original photo as it blends in with the dark base of the temporary barrier. It also appears small. The witness measured the metal fencing to the right of the animal at five feet high and fifteen feet from the temporary barrier. While I was unable to visit the site, I have measured multiple stakes used to create similar temporary barriers in the area around my home. They have all measured right at four feet in height. Based on these measurements, the cat in this photo is approaching four feet in length from nose to tail. The cat is very long-bodied and lean, much like a jaguarundi. Another interesting aspect to this photo is that the cat appears to be carrying something in its mouth. Could it be a cub/kitten? It is entirely possible the cat in the Ray Hubbard photo is a domestic/feral, but if so, it is quite a big one.

132 Shadow Cats

This photo was reportedly taken by trail camera near Columbia, South Carolina. It could show a jaguarundi. (Texas Cryptid Hunter)

I have very little information on this photo. This is something of a common theme, I know. A reader of the *Texas Cryptid Hunter* website shared this photo with me and said only that it was taken via a trail camera outside of Columbia, South Carolina. Follow-up questions went unanswered, so all we have is the photo. It certainly appears, based on the hardwood tree and leaf litter, like the picture could have been taken in South Carolina. For that matter, the vegetation is reminiscent of wooded areas all across the South. Clearly, the photo has been cropped and zoomed, as there are none of the usual date and time stamps present on game camera photos. Scale is difficult to assess, but we do have that tree just behind the cat to help us with this matter. I cannot say what the diameter of that tree might be, but it is clearly no sapling. If we assume the tree measures somewhere between one-and-a-half feet and two feet from left edge to right edge, the cat would measure somewhere in the three-and-a-half to four-foot range from the tip of the tail to the nose. This cat really has a jaguarundi look about it, in my opinion. It is long-bodied and has a very long tail. Most tellingly, the head appears flat and sloping, otter-like. While there is a bit of thin vegetation in the foreground that obscures a totally clean view of the head, I do not feel it is thick enough to create this illusion. While this is not a photo of a huge cat, it is bigger than a typical domestic/feral and could be a jaguarundi. If so, it is an important piece of evidence suggesting that these elusive and rare cats have expanded their range considerably.

*This photo was taken via trail camera near Burnet, Texas.
(Matt Rhyner)*

This photo was sent in by a gentleman named Matt Rhyner on March 30, 2017. The image was captured near a deer feeder on his grandfather's property near Burnet, Texas. I have shown this photo to several wildlife experts, and they are divided as to what is shown in the picture. Some feel that it is a photo of a large black cat, while others speculate it might be two piglets standing close together. Again, interesting but inconclusive.

This large black cat was photographed near Lake LBJ in central Texas and was estimated to be roughly the size of a female Weimaraner.
(Terry "Tex" Tolar)

This photo was snapped near Horseshoe Bay on Lake LBJ in central Texas. The photographer spotted the feline from his truck and, initially, felt he was seeing a big dog. As he slowed his vehicle to get a better look, the animal sped up and made its getaway. The witness has worked on ranches all over Texas his entire life and has seen mountain lions, bobcats, and jaguarundis; he is adamant that the cat he saw was something else. The cat is long-bodied with powerful hips. The head, however, appears too small to be that of a true big cat. The witness estimated the cat was approximately 40 lbs. and almost as tall as his female Weimaraner, but longer. Female Weimaraners average about 24 inches in height and 55-60 lbs. in weight. If the witness is accurate in his estimates, this was a sizeable cat. The witness added: "I really would have thought it an escaped black panther. It had that stride of a big cat."

Photographic Evidence   135

A pair of cat-like animals pass in front of a deer feeder. Note the distinctive J-posture of the tail exhibited by the smaller animal.
(Jeff Stewart)

Jeff Stewart, a noted east Texas outdoorsman, shared this final photo with me. He featured the picture in a presentation at the PhilosoPhenomena Unity Fest in March of 2015. The photo clearly shows two large black animals walking by a deer feeder. The assumption here is that we are looking at a mother and her cub, but it is impossible to say with absolute certainty that we are looking at two cats here. Many argue that the larger animal could be a dog of some kind. The fact that the animal is on the move and slightly out of focus – not to mention the fact that what I have is a photo of the original picture up on a computer screen – makes it very difficult to say for sure. It is the smaller animal, however, that really makes me lean toward the pair being felids of some kind. The tail of the smaller animal is curled in the classic J-shape so often reported by witnesses. This is something that can clearly be seen to some degree in almost every photo included in this chapter. The cub, assuming that is what it is, is very thick, even chubby. I cannot say why that would be, but that tail is very cat-like. Regardless, the photo is extremely interesting and worthy of inclusion in this roundup of alleged black panther photographs.

A trail camera photo from the American South. Big dog or big cat?
(Texas Cryptid Hunter)

This photo is both tantalizing and frustrating. I am told the picture was originally submitted to *Field & Stream* as part of a photo contest but cannot confirm that. I have no backstory other than that. According to the time stamp, the photo was taken in September of 2010. The reader who sent it to me added that it was taken in the American South. The animal in the photo has a powerful and thick build, as well as the shiny black coat that witnesses often mention, but it cannot be positively identified due to the fact that its head is obscured by a tree. Once again, interesting but inconclusive.

The photos presented in this chapter, as well as those seen previously, are simply not enough to prove the existence of a breeding population of black, long-tailed cats of panther-sized proportions in the American South. The photos do, however, provide some very interesting anecdotal evidence that there is a living, breathing, biological entity behind black panther sightings here in North America. Some of the photos in this book feature animals that are clearly large and muscular, while others show creatures that are small and slender. This discrepancy in size and shape is often a bone of contention among skeptics. They believe if there really was such an animal as a black panther, the appearance would be more uniform. That might be true if there was only one species of animal behind the black panther enigma, something I am not so sure about (more about that in Chapter 15). What is clear is that there are quite a few large black cats roaming around in the woods of Texas and the American South.

My hope is that these photos and this book will intrigue wildlife authorities enough that they will be compelled to look into this mystery and find out exactly what is stalking the more rural areas of the South.

13

The Texas Hair Samples

IT IS SIMPLY A FACT that photos or videos are not going to be enough to prove the existence of a large, black, long-tailed cat in Texas. With the advent of digital technology, even a rank amateur has the capability to produce a convincing hoaxed photo. It has also become common for a legitimate photo to float around cyberspace long enough that the original backstory of the picture is lost. These photos make the rounds via the internet and social media and can cause quite a stir.

This photo has made the rounds on the internet. The back story most often given is that it was taken in central Texas, but it was actually taken in South Africa. (Kevin Richardson)

One such photo, which I have had to debunk at least a dozen times, is a photo of a melanistic leopard walking past a game camera. According to the story I was given, the photo was taken in central Texas near the small town of Kosse. The photo is real enough, but it was not taken anywhere near central Texas. The picture was taken by a Mr. Kevin Richardson and shows a melanistic leopard living in captivity. The photo accompanied an article called "Chasing Mpumalanga's Black Leopard" on the *Nelspruit News* website.[198]

One of the first things I look for in an effort to determine if a photo is genuine is whether or not the vegetation in the picture fits the alleged location. Most people focus so much on the subject of the photo that they fail to consider other details visible in the frame like plants and trees. In this case there was nothing in the photo proving it could not have been captured in central Texas. That being the case, I moved on to another of my debunking strategies: a simple internet image search. After entering "black panther photos" into my favorite search engine, it did not take long for me to find this exact photograph and the link to the *Nelspruit News* story. The truth about the photo was revealed easily enough but did require just a little digging, something most people are not likely to do. The whole episode illustrates why a photo, or even a video, alone will never be enough to prove that a cat, which is not supposed to exist, does in fact exist. Solid physical evidence will be required to prove the existence of black panthers, whatever they may turn out to be in North America; however, no such evidence exists.

Or does it?

On January 31, 2013, I received an email from a reader of the *Texas Cryptid Hunter* website. He claimed that, two nights previously, he had hit what he described as a very large, black cat on Highway 90 just south of Madisonville, Texas. He described the incident in his email of 2013:

> Last night I was traveling back from Houston to Dallas on the back roads to avoid traffic. Around 9:00 p.m. I was on HWY 90 south of Madisonville and hit a large black cat with my car. The animal was by my estimation about 80 lbs. and bigger than my English springer spaniel. I was travel-

ing about 70 mph with high beams on, it was clear, and I could see fine. But suddenly from the left side of the road it appeared and stopped just in front of the car, and turned to look at me.

There appeared to be embankments on each side of the road and I discounted swerving or going into the ditch to avoid it, so I hit the brakes hard. As I did the animal turned to face me and I saw clearly two blue eyes reflected back at me by my lights, and a clear feline face and large body. I think by the time I hit it the car had slowed to about 30-35 mph. There was a thud on impact, but I didn't 'run over it,' I think it went under the car. I pulled over about 50 yards farther and paused to take a look at the damage on my car. The front quarter panel was torn up and there were some fluids leaking and I noted some vapor clouds that smelled of radiator coolant. I determined that I needed to get into town ASAP before the car was no longer drivable.

When in town I assessed the damage and had to tie up parts and put extra fluid in the car and was eventually able to nurse it back to Dallas where I live.

When I got home my wife and I did some research and I am convinced I saw and hit a black panther. I grew up in the Huntsville area and as a teen heard stories of people seeing them in the area.

This morning just before the car was towed away I inspected it again and found a collection of long semi-soft black hairs that had become stuck in the plastic. I have these and put them in a baggie. I am writing this to you to ask for any insight or ideas on how I can determine if, indeed, this was a black panther or if my eyes deceived me and it was perhaps a wild hog, or, possibly, a coyote. I am so sure that the face and head was that of a large feline, and I am mad now that I didn't try to go look in the ditch for it, but I feared my car was failing and didn't want to tangle with a large wounded animal should I find it. Any ideas?

I replied to this gentleman and asked if he could provide a more specific location of the incident. He wrote:

> The location was on Hwy 90, south of Madisonville, and just north of the County Road 106 cut off. As best I can recall, I know I had just crossed some small bridge and the road side was dropping off sharp, or appeared when I saw the animal which, and looking at the maps on Google, I think the incident happened somewhere between the two little bridges you can see on Google maps.

I immediately contacted a friend who lives within an hour of the alleged accident site and asked if he could go inspect the area and look for any sign that could confirm the story. My friend conducted a thorough inspection of the area and took lots of photos. But he was unable to find any sign that a large animal had been struck in the area "between the two little bridges" and even ventured a bit further up and down the road on either side of the two bridges in the hopes of finding something. He had no luck. It should be noted, however, that he was not able to get too deep into the wood line just off the highway as it was fenced (barbed wire) and privately owned. It is not outside the realm of possibility that whatever this witness struck with his vehicle managed to get into those woods before recovering or expiring.

After I informed the witness that a search of the accident site had not yielded any evidence, he agreed to send me the hairs he had collected from the damaged front end of his vehicle. My hope was that these hairs could be submitted for analysis and provide insight into what creature might be responsible for black panther sightings in the Lone Star State. The entire prospect was quite exciting. I realized that there was a good chance that these hairs would turn out to be from something mundane, but I had high hopes that I had been provided with evidence that might, if not prove, at least support the possibility that there are large black cats of some kind living in Texas.

The first thing I decided to do was to get the hairs to Mark Mc-

Clurken, a friend of mine who has some background in hair analysis. To be completely up front, Mark is not a professional when it comes to this sort of thing but is very competent, owns his own microscope, and has the know-how to quickly identify the hair of most common North American mammals. He holds a degree in Animal Science from Tarleton State University and is a lifelong hunter, trapper, naturalist, and a self-confessed "lab rat." He is more than qualified to do the initial analysis of these hairs. I wanted to make sure that I didn't have a bag full of hog hair before I went out on a limb and sent the samples in to a university or lab for analysis.

Mark's findings were promising, as he found both undercoat and guard hairs among the samples. His initial email to me regarding the hair samples stated, in part:

> I got a scale cast on the same hair from the undercoat. Thankfully, we didn't have to waste that sample. The hairs from the undercoat look like cat to me. The guard hairs are tougher. They are so thick and dark that I can't see the medulla with this microscope. I'll try doing a scale cast on one tomorrow to see if the pattern matches the undercoat. I'm a bit paranoid, but I wouldn't put it past someone to throw both dog and cat hairs in a bag to see what we do. However, from a quick glance, the scale pattern appears to be overlapping nicely on the edge of the guard hairs too.

A second email from Mark soon followed:

> So far, it still has potential, because the cuticle has an acuminate imbricate pattern and the medulla appears to be uniserial on the fleece. If I see that on the guard hair, then we might want to have someone confirm what I'm seeing, especially if they have a polarizing microscope.

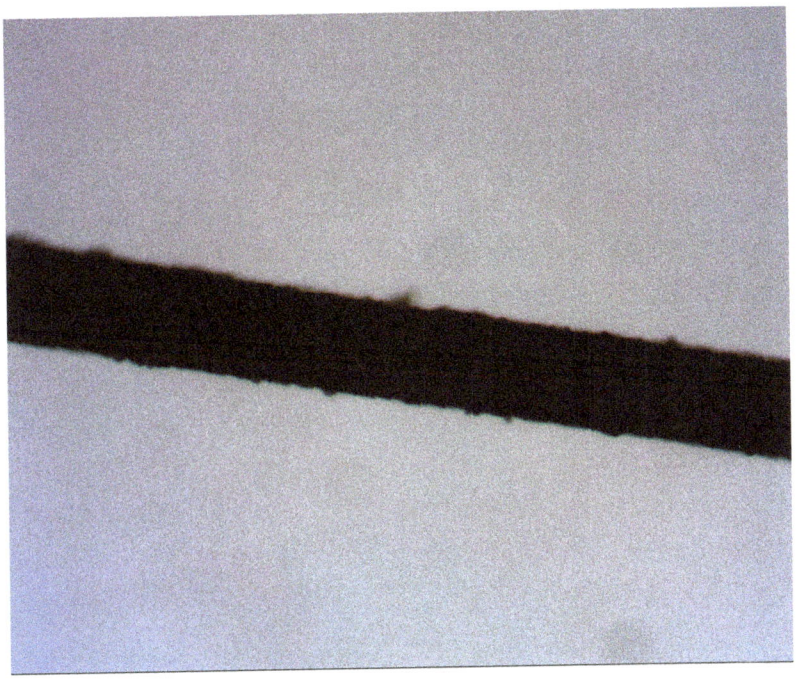

Guard hair shaft magnified x 40.
(Mark McClurken)

The next conversation centered around the possibility of misidentification. Could the gentleman who struck the animal have made a mistake? Could the animal have been something common? Assuming the witness was right, and the animal weighed in the 80 lbs. range, there are a limited number of candidates from which to choose that might have been mistaken for a large cat. In my mind, the list is limited to a feral hog, coyote (though it would be a huge one), mountain lion, or large breed of domestic dog. Mark's response was as follows:

> It's definitely not a hog, that's 100% certain. I'm still working on the dog aspect. I just want to make sure. As for domestic cat vs. wild one, that is something you can usually rule out by the other characteristics of the hair, such as diameter. The guard hairs are the ones

> I'm really looking at closely right now. Melanistic cats of any kind aren't really uncommon. Those guard hairs are awfully thick for most small cats, though. Truth be told, it looks a heck of a lot like leopard hair…

*Hair shaft magnified x 40.
(Mark McClurken)*

A little later, Mark wrote again:

> It looks a whole lot like these leopard hairs. These are using a special microscope, so they look a bit different than what I'm seeing, but the structure is the same. Look at the medulla running through the center of the shaft. Notice how they look like single file stacked

disks? That's a uniserial pattern. You don't see that
in dogs. The fleece hairs look like this except that the
medulla is black and the cortex and cuticle are dark
brown. Which would make the hair appear black.
See the very small notches on the side of the hair that
look like they are overlapping at pretty even intervals?
That is the cuticle. Your fleece hairs have a similar
pattern.

Now really intrigued, Mark dug into a copy of the *Atlas and Key to the Hair of Terrestrial Texas Mammals* supplied to me by a professor at Texas Tech University. Nothing he found there changed his mind that these samples likely came from a cat of some kind. He then sent me his final remarks on the case:

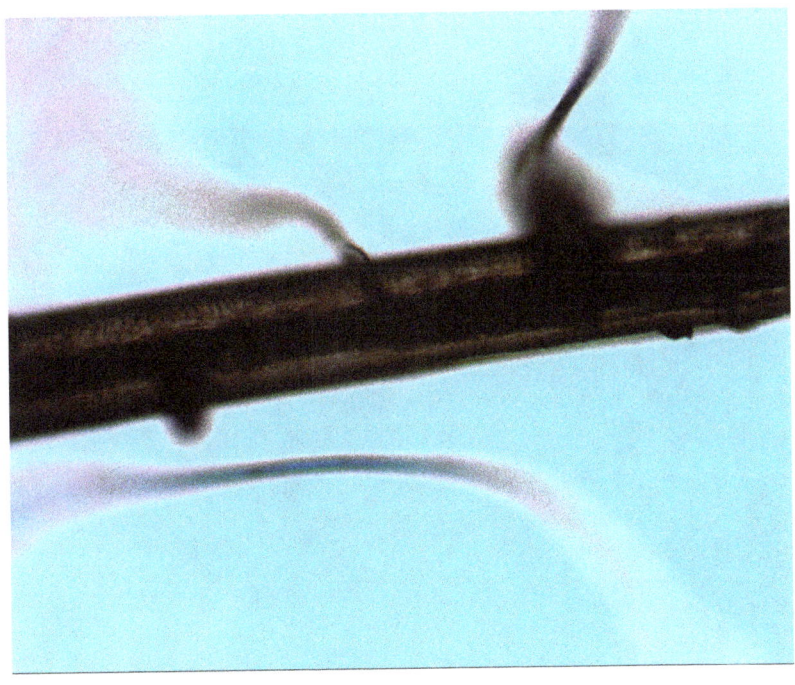

Guard hair magnified x 40.
(Mark McClurken)

> Your particular hairs are pretty interesting. The scale pattern isn't all that remarkable. You can see it in cats and even in some dogs. The medulla is where it starts to get interesting. The medulla is really broad, is distinctly uniserial, and is more complex in the guard hairs. Throw in the fact that the hairs are visually black, which means a dark medulla and red edges under a scope, and they need someone with a better grasp to look at them. One thing you might try is forensics labs rather than wildlife folks but I still think that it is cat hair after looking at the key.

Encouraged, I set about contacting the biology departments of various Texas universities. I included the photos of the hair samples, as well as the comments made by Mark during his initial analysis. I was confident that, if nothing else, enough had been done to convince someone at one of these universities to take a look at these samples. I was wrong.

Guard hair root magnified x 40.
(Mark McClurken)

Most of my inquiries went unanswered. I suppose my request was not even deemed worthy of a polite dismissal. I received one reply in which a professor, who seemed somewhat annoyed, lectured me on the fact that "black panthers do not exist." He mentioned that there was zero evidence supporting their existence, and there was "simply no such thing."

I did receive a nice email from a professor at Texas A&M who put out my request on some sort of academic forum. This was somewhat beneficial in that it resulted in a professor from Texas Tech University sending me the copy of the hair atlas mentioned previously. No one, however, expressed a willingness to actually examine the samples.

I received only two replies expressing any interest whatsoever. Both of these replies came from the respective heads of their university's biology departments. Both said they would forward my request to their mammologists. One of the two even regaled me with the story of his own black panther sighting in southeast Texas a few years previously. As you can imagine, I was very encouraged by this development and excitedly awaited further word from either of these two.

It did not happen. I waited one week, then two. Nothing. Finally, I emailed them both again and politely asked if they had spoken with their colleagues regarding the hair samples. This time, only one of them replied, the one who claimed to have had a sighting himself. His tone had changed dramatically from our first conversation in which he was friendly and gregarious. His response to my second query was curt, and he seemed more than a bit annoyed that I had contacted him again. He said only, "It would do you no good for me to look at the samples." I pointed out in a final email that he had mentioned discussing the matter with his mammologist and asked if that conversation had occurred. His one sentence reply said he would speak to the gentleman. Weeks turned to months and months to years without my hearing anything. It is pretty clear that I never will.

I find myself in a rather ironic situation. I have been told by biologists that there is no such thing as a black panther. This is the official position of mainstream science due to the fact that, to this date, no evidence has been found to support their existence. When I have shared with these scientists that I may very well have evidence that could support the existence of a large, black, long-tailed cat in Texas, I am told that my evidence cannot be valid since the animal does not exist. The circular nature of these arguments is incredibly frustrating.

I would like to stress that I have never asked any individual or university to run DNA tests on these hair samples. I realize that these tests are time consuming and expensive. I would never ask anyone else to foot the bill for something like that. All I have ever asked is that someone with experience in wildlife hair analysis and morphology take a look at these samples under a microscope. All that would take is a bit of time, and it would not cost any individual or university a single dime. I could then make a decision on whether or not to attempt DNA extraction and testing, at my expense, based on the results of this initial analysis. Despite this, all of my requests have fallen on deaf ears, and no one to date has agreed to examine these hair samples. I am hopeful that will change, but until then the samples continue to languish in an envelope tucked in a bedside drawer in my home.

14

The Experts Weigh In

We have thus far discussed historical ranges, folklore, old and contemporary sightings, habitat, melanism, and the most probable suspects in the black panther mystery. What has not yet been discussed in detail is what wildlife experts think about the possibility that large, black, long-tailed cats roam the Lone Star State and other parts of the American South. In an attempt to rectify this situation, I sought out people experienced with big cats and solicited their input. I created a big cat questionnaire and sent it out to experts all over the country. While the response rate was disappointingly low, the experts who did agree to participate are of the highest quality, and I could not be more pleased that they have agreed to share their opinions on this matter.

Here are the six experts queried, their academic and/or professional credentials, and areas of specialization:

- Amy Rodrigues is a zoologist. She had been employed for the last nine years as a biologist for the Mountain Lion Foundation (MLF), a national nonprofit dedicated to protecting *Puma concolor* and its habitat.

- Michelle Schireman is a zookeeper with thirty years of experience, currently employed by the Oregon Zoo. She has been the AZA North America Regional Studbook keeper for Puma for the last twenty-five years, and AZA Species Population Manager for Puma.

- Chester Moore is the editor-in-chief for *Texas Fish & Game* magazine. He is has been a wildlife journalist and researcher for twenty-four years, and is the owner and director of Kingdom Zoo Wildlife Center, a USDA licensed facility.

- Lisa Werner is director of Programs and Services at Tiger Creek Wildlife Refuge, a USDA licensed facility.

- Jim Broaddus is director and owner of Bear Creek Feline Center, a USDA licensed facility.

- Jeff Stewart is a contributor to *Texas Fish & Game* magazine, has done advanced studies in Animal Science, is a Veterinary Technician, and is a Research Assistant at Southern Panther Search.

I asked each of these experts the same fifteen questions. Here are the questions and their replies.

Mainstream science does not recognize the existence of a large, black, long-tailed cat, commonly referred to as a black panther, in North America. Yet, people in Texas and across the south report seeing such an animal on a fairly regular basis. Do you have any thoughts as to what could explain these sightings?

Rodrigues: More than 80% of mountain lion sightings are false (typically house cats or other animals moving quickly through the brush from a distance), and this is a species with well-documented populations in the American West. Black panther sightings are likely the same type of misidentification and eyes playing tricks on the viewer. In places where people have never seen a mountain lion, it's even easier to forget just how big they actually are and accidentally mistake a large house cat for its much larger cousin.

Schireman: I cannot explain the reports, but I wonder how far away the cat was from the reporter. I often get reports of pumas in rural areas that end up being house cats. They are far from the people, so their size is over estimated.

Moore: I think many are mistaken identity such as dogs and other animals. Others are cougars seen in lowlight conditions. Still others could be jaguarundis or, possibly, melanistic jaguars.

Werner: I believe people are seeing a large black exotic cat in the south, but it is my opinion that what they are actually seeing are the jaguarundis or a jaguar.

Broaddus: Melanistic *Puma concolor*. I have seen one myself. I know it was a puma, as I train them, work with them, and exhibit them. I know what a puma looks like.

Stewart: Science does not recognize a black long-tailed cat in the U.S., though the jaguar once roamed much of what are now the southern states. The jaguarundi is not necessarily a large cat and not actually black but dark grey. It is my theory that interbreeding between domestic cats and bobcats and jaguarundis have produced dark-colored offspring with long tails. A dark-colored cat the size of a bobcat would seem enormous if viewed for a split second in fading light. With the influx of feral hogs into much of the South, including Mexico and South America, it is not much of a stretch to say jaguars might have followed the hogs, which follow the rivers and streams, north into Texas. There are many logical explanations for the sightings of large black cats which do not include the popular black cougar theory.

*

Have you had people report black panther sightings to you directly? If so, how did you respond?

Rodrigues: Yes, I receive approximately one report every month or two of a black panther somewhere in the U.S. For comparison, I also receive reports daily of lion sightings or signs of their presence (tracks, scat, scratches, caterwauls, etc.). I have never received any solid evidence, though, of a black panther. I usually respond with the science and explain there is no documented proof of a melanistic mountain lion. An escaped exotic pet such as a black leopard or black jaguar is technically possible, but rare. Mountain lions can look darker under low light and from certain angles. I always recommend people install motion-activated cameras to catch of glimpse of what critters are prowling their property at night. Although lion sightings in the east are very rare, and no evidence of a black panther has ever been found, photos are a great way to objectively review these reported cases.

Schireman: No.

Moore: I have probably gathered 500 reports in 24 years, and I respond by asking questions about their sighting.

Werner: I have had people report to me having seen a large black exotic cat in East Texas, and my husband and I both saw one ourselves a few years back, and we both believe what we saw was a melanistic Jaguar.

Broaddus: Yes, I have. I thank them for trusting me enough to share and then question them on the where, when, time, light conditions, distance, etc. I am always glad to hear a report because I know they do exist.

Stewart: I have received many reports of black panthers. My own parents have had several sightings over the years. I always take these reports in earnest.

*

Do you feel it is possible that jaguars are slowly returning to their historical range, which would include Texas and much of the southeastern United States?

Rodrigues: If we stop killing jaguars and protect their habitat, wildlife corridors, and prey, they absolutely could return to the U.S. I followed the story of Macho B when he crossed into Arizona a few years back and his unfortunate death. As of February 2016, there was a jaguar back in the U.S. just outside Tucson. Like mountain lions, female jaguars don't disperse far from their birthplace so it will take more generations before a female is likely to show up in our country, and ultimately help establish a breeding population. Until then, we will likely continue to see bachelors pass through in search of a mate. Hunters and poachers could easily prevent the species' recovery though.

Schireman: I hope so and I believe that they are slowly recovering.

Moore: I do think so. It's proven in New Mexico and Arizona.

Werner: Absolutely.

Broaddus: Yes, based on conversations with colleagues. Other wildlife from Central and South America drifts north through Mexico and into the United States so, why not jaguars?

Stewart: I do believe that the jaguar may be returning to its former home.

*

Jaguars do exhibit melanism on occasion (some estimate as many as 1 out of 10 jaguars exhibit partial or complete melanism, which seems high to me). In your experience, is this an accurate percentage?

Rodrigues: I am not familiar enough with melanism rates to contribute a helpful response to this question. My guess is that, like white tigers, some of these traits that are rare in the wild are more commonly seen in captive animals because of selective breeding.

Schireman: No question about melanism in jags. I am not sure what you mean by "partial melanism." One in ten seems very high.

Moore: I did an interview with a biologist from Panthera, the research group - not to be confused with Pantera, the defunct metal band, lol. He told me new research shows that melanism is a dominant trait in jaguars, so if there was a remnant in say – Texas - and they were melanistic, it stands to reason remaining cats could be melanistic as well.

Werner: I think that percentage seems high. However, Tiger Creek was home to a melanistic jaguar named 8-ball for quite some time. Before we rescued him, he was owned as a pet and kept chained up in a bar as a side attraction. He provided a great opportunity for us to discuss melanism in big cats and to address the black panther myth.

Broaddus: I am not familiar enough with the topic to say. I would only be speculating if I answered.

Stewart: I believe that cross breeding of many cat species has led to many of the reported sightings. I also believe the rate of melanism may be slightly higher than reported in jaguars.

*

Do you feel that mountain lions have expanded their breeding population beyond the generally accepted range in deep south Texas and far west Texas? If so, do you feel that mountain lions could be responsible for the black panther sightings in Texas?

Rodrigues: I don't believe breeding populations have expanded much between south/western Texas and the Florida everglades. Dispersing male lions have been known to wander hundreds and even thousands of miles (i.e. the lion shot by police in Chicago or the one road kill in Connecticut or recent Tennessee confirmation are all famous long-distance trekkers). These cats can account for some of the panther sightings (whether black or tan) in states without known breeding populations but, from my experience, most sightings are still other animals like house cats, dogs, bobcats, coyotes, and deer. Check out the Cougar Network's confirmations map for proven/documented lion sightings.

Schireman: Yes, I think they may be expanding their territory. It is possible that pumas are being misidentified as being black, possibly due to poor lighting.

Moore: The idea that *Felis concolor*, the mountain lion/cougar/puma/panther/catamount, has ever been relegated to south and west Texas is a myth. They are indigenous to the Lower 48, into Canada and down south to Argentina. There have been population ups and downs, but cougars, as I tend to call them, have always been beyond the west/south Texas region here in my home state.

Werner: We do have mountain lions in Texas, and I think that is the reason for people assuming that the large black cat they are seeing it a "panther." However, I think that in addition to the mountain lion we also have jaguarundis and jaguars.

Broaddus: Yes and no. You see, they have always been there. Certainly, the populations are more concentrated in some areas, but *Puma concolor* has always been found across the country though numbers have dwindled due to various factors.

Stewart: Mountain lions, without a doubt, have expanded their ranges. Many verifiable trail camera photos have surfaced over the past few years which show cougars in Panola and other east Texas counties.

*

Is it correct that there has never been a melanistic mountain lion documented? Do you believe it is possible that mountain lions could exhibit melanism on rare occasions?

Rodrigues: Correct. To my knowledge, there has never been a documented case of a melanistic mountain lion. I've seen lions with slightly darker fur, and kittens that look almost solid gray, but never a black adult mountain lion. I think it could be possible, but clearly not a trait or mutation that occurs at some recordable frequency like melanism or albinism do in other wildlife species.

Schireman: There have been no documented (photographed) black pumas. I do not think they exhibit melanism or someone would have photographed one.

Moore: Yes, that is true. There is a really old black and white photo floating around of a killed cougar that looks really dark brown from Costa Rica but it is unconfirmed. I do not think melanism is probable. If you look at the cats of the world, only the spotted ones exhibit melanism - none in lions, caracals, etc.

Werner: It is my belief that there have not been documented cases of melanistic mountain lions. It is my understanding and belief that it is not genetically possible for a *Felis concolor* to produce a melanistic offspring.

Broaddus: It is correct that there are no photos or a specimen of a melanistic puma, but I do not think it is impossible. Wild cats have no Jane Goodall out there studying them intensely. How can we really know for sure?

Stewart: There are many older photos showing dark-colored

cougars but no black ones. I do believe there is a possibility of black as a color in cougars due to possible cross-breeding with other cat species that do carry the gene for melanism.

*

Does the color of a typical mountain lion's coat get darker or lighter depending on the time of year? For example, does the coat get darker in the winter months when it thickens up?

Rodrigues: I can't speak for the pigment changing, but there is some evidence suggested in *Cougar: The American Lion* that the lion's coat is "short year-round in warmer climates but grows longer and thicker during the winter in temperate regions." It seems unlikely the overall color and appearance of the cat would change substantially. Likely, they are just larger and fluffier in Canada, and smaller with shorter hair near the equator.

Schireman: Not that I know of.

Moore: I wouldn't think so.

Werner: To my knowledge, the coat does not change color with the seasons.

Broaddus: Coats do vary in coloration, thickness, and length somewhat based on region, but there really are no color variations due to seasonal changes.

Stewart: The color of a cougar's coat may vary during certain times of the year due to the act of bedding in hardwood leaf litter, which has tannins that leach out of the leaves and into the fur of the cat.

*

Is it possible that jaguarundis have expanded their breeding populations beyond their generally accepted range in South and Central America, Mexico, and occasionally, extreme south Texas? If so, could jaguarundis be responsible for the black panther sightings in Texas?

Rodrigues: I have not heard anything about a growing jaguarundi population in the U.S. Escaped captives could be mistaken for any number of other species including lions, house cats, weasels, fishers, otters, and even monkeys. The jaguarundi is small, and anyone mistaking it for a black panther could just as easily confuse a large black house cat for a panther.

Schireman: This is possible, but they are not all that much bigger than house cats! Maybe the sightings are house cats?

Moore: Yes, they could, and I think they have been in these areas for a long time.

Werner: Yes, I believe they are one of the reasons for the sightings, but I believe the main culprit is the jaguar.

Broaddus: Absolutely, no doubt about it.

Stewart: Jaguarundis can definitely be one of the explanations for sightings of black panthers.

*

Jaguarundi coloration varies quite a bit (charcoal grey, rusty red, brown, black). Do individual jaguarundis go through all of these color phases, or are individual cats simply born one color or the other and remain that way for life?

Rodrigues: Not something I'm familiar with.

Schireman: Born that color and remain that color. I have taken care of several.

Moore: They come in different color phases like fallow deer, which come in white, spotted, and chocolate.

Werner: I have not had any direct experience with the jaguarundi to speculate if the coat changes color over time.

Broaddus: They are born a certain color and remain that color for life. No changes.

Stewart: Jaguarundis are, generally, one phase but may get darker with age. Different color phases can be seen in jaguarundis from the same litter.

*

It is generally accepted that an adult male jaguarundi will weigh between 20-25 lbs. and measure 45-60 inches in length (including the tail). Do you feel these estimates are correct? Have you heard of or seen any significantly larger specimens?

Rodrigues: Not something I'm too familiar with, but your estimates seem to be on the larger side already, and I've never heard of a larger jaguarundi. I've seen two, in captivity, who were both around 12 lbs.

Schireman: Sounds right for the weight, but that length seems a little large. I've never seen one out of that range.

Moore: That is about right, but many are actually much smaller.

Werner: I have not had any direct experience with jaguarundis.

Broaddus: Those estimates are a bit on the large side, but, yes, generally they are about right. My captive cats tend to be a bit heavier than wild specimens. (I have a male that weighs 28 lbs.) I am unaware of any jaguarundis reaching significantly larger sizes either in captivity or in the wild.

Stewart: Most jaguarundis do not get heavier than 20 lbs., with 25 lbs. being a cat of extremely large size. Cross breeding could explain sightings of larger-sized cats.

*

My research has revealed claims that jaguarundis have been documented in Florida and coastal Alabama. Is this true? If so, in your opinion, how did they get there? Could there be a population of jaguarundis, though small in number, stretching all along the Gulf Coast?

Rodrigues: This is news to me. If they turn up in the U.S., there's a chance, like the jaguar, they dispersed on their own. There is also a good chance they were illegal pets escaped or released into the wild. Capturing one and running a DNA test would help.

Schireman: I doubt it. I think they were escaped pets, like some of the Florida panther stock.

Moore: I wouldn't say "verified" because state officials won't accept it, but I do believe they are there. My friend Jim *Broaddus* with Bear Creek Feline Center does great work on this topic and has a breeding population of jaguarundis at his place. He is the expert on the subject in my opinion.

Broaddus: True, they are here in Florida, and I think there is likely a small and fragile breeding population along the Gulf Coast. I am unsure how they might have arrived, but human introduction seems the most likely explanation.

Werner: I think that over time exotic animals adapt, due to the process of habitat destruction, and it is possible for them to migrate to sustain themselves.

Stewart: I have also heard of jaguarundi sightings in other states and have seen trail camera photos associated with these reports. I do believe that jaguarundis have traveled by way of rivers and streams to those states.

*

Of late, numerous articles originating in Australia have referenced the documentation of feral cats that have reached unusually large sizes. Do you feel that something similar could be occurring here in the United States?

Rodrigues: Anything is possible, and there is a feral cat problem in the U.S. However, it seems to me that if cats were getting exceptionally large, there would be more proof (captured individuals, road kill, trail-camera images, etc.) to substantiate the claims. Without natural predators, individuals in a species can grow larger over time and many generations. In most of the South, even though there are no wolves, lions, or brown bears, smaller carnivores like coyotes, bobcats, and feral dogs are likely to prey on feral cats and prevent them from evolving into a larger subspecies. I'm not sure what other parameters have led to Australia's feral cats getting so big, but I have seen some of these reports.

Schireman: I don't think so, but consider the source. When it comes to Australia and carnivores, there is no love lost.

Moore: Sure. I have seen a couple of really big feral cats.

Werner: I believe there are larger feral cats, but I do not believe this is the origination of the black panther sightings.

Broaddus: Ferals are mean and aggressive so they tend to do quite well. Anything doing well is unlikely to grow smaller over time so, it is possible they are getting bigger.

Stewart: I do believe that feral cats have attained a larger size and are responsible for some sightings in Australia and the U.S.

*

Often, wildlife experts speculate that a black panther sighting is the result of an escaped or released exotic pet such as a leopard. Are you aware of any documented incidents where a black panther was reported and an exotic of this nature was actually found, captured, or killed?

Rodrigues: [Ms. *Rodrigues* did not answer the question directly but provided a link to a *Huffington Post* article detailing the shooting of a leopard in Indiana: "Leopard Shot, Killed By Indiana Man Did Not Belong To Wildlife Refuge" http://www.huffingtonpost.com/2013/06/24/leopard-killed-indiana-video_n_3491338.html.]

Schireman: I guess I am confused. When I hear black panther, I am thinking black leopard. I realize there are black jaguar and black serval and smaller cats, but when I hear black panther that is my assumption. Are you aware of all the "sightings" in the UK? I believe they ended up being released or missing pets.

Moore: No, not a single case.

Werner: No.

Broaddus: No.

Stewart: I know of no verified circumstance where an escaped exotic was killed after a sighting of a black panther.

*

Do you have any knowledge as to how many exotic cats are kept as pets in the United States and/or Texas? Are there any special permits required to own an exotic big cat such as a leopard?

Rodrigues: MLF doesn't focus much on captivity issues, other than rescue and rehab of wild lions. Try organizations like Born Free or Big Cat Rescue for stats and laws on exotic species in the U.S.: http://bigcatrescue.org/state-laws-exotic-cats/.
Mountain lions can be kept in Texas. For info on the laws and regulations, see the "Captivity" section near the bottom of http://www.mountainlion.org/us/tx/-tx-portal.asp.

Schireman: There are numbers out there. The Feline Conservation Federation can give you better numbers from their members who are private owners of exotics. YES, you are required to hold permits and meet certain standards in the U.S. The laws vary by state, county, and city.

Moore: There is no survey but the numbers in private ownership are vastly down in comparison to the 1990s.

Werner: There is not an accurate number as to how many people have exotics as pets in Texas. There are many professional groups that have attempted to create a registry, but not everyone notifies the registry of changes in the numbers. It is a requirement to be licensed by the USDA in order to have big cats in captivity in Texas. Unfortunately, there are always people who do not follow the rules and obtain these cats illegally. This adds to the registry numbers being inaccurate.

Broaddus: I do not know. The USDA might have those numbers. I do know regulations vary wildly state to state and, sometimes, even county to county. Overall, though, the government has done everything it can to discourage the ownership of exotic big cats. Due to increased regulation and political pressure, the number of people keeping Type I big cats has dwindled significantly.

Stewart: As a teen, I worked for a man who raised various types of big cats for circuses. As far as I know, it takes special permits and/or licenses to own big cats.

*

In your opinion, is it possible that there is an undocumented species of big cat existing in Texas and/or the southern United States that could account for black panther sightings?

Rodrigues: Science has surprised me enough over the years that I believe anything is possible. However, at this time, I don't think it's probable an undocumented species of big cat exists in the United States. There are so many people and trail cameras on the landscape, a breeding population of a large feline would have been documented by now. I'm more than happy to be proven wrong though! Keep those eyes open and cameras ready!

Schireman: No.

Moore: Undocumented as in an "unknown" species? No. I believe all cat sightings can be explained by native species with some possible hybridization among them.

Werner: No.

Broaddus: No, I think there are melanistic pumas and that is what people are likely seeing.

Stewart: In my opinion, the sightings of large black cats can be attributed to known species or hybrids produced by cross breeding.

*

While the experts questioned differed somewhat in their opinions over the course of the survey, for the most part they remained on the same page. For example, none believe there is an undocumented species of large, black, long-tailed cat living in Texas and the southern United States. All feel that black panther sightings can be explained by a combination of visuals of common native species (cougar), uncommon native species (jaguar and jaguarundi), domestic/feral cats, or escaped exotics. Mr. Stewart added one more possibility with his theory that at least some sightings might be explained by the offspring of domestic/ferals and jaguarundi. Most also mentioned that misidentifications were common occurrences when it comes to big cat sightings.

The experts did diverge slightly when it came to the animal most likely being seen by witnesses. Mr. Moore and Ms. Werner felt that jaguars and jaguarundis were strong candidates with Mr. Moore leaning more on the jaguarundi side of the matter and Ms. Werner believing it is more likely witnesses have seen jaguars. Ms. Rodrigues and Ms. Schireman indicated that they believe most sightings of black panthers have likely been cases of mistaken identity or escaped exotics, while Mr. Broaddus, based largely on his own visual of a large black puma-like cat and discussions with colleagues who have worked in the Amazon basin, stated a belief that it is probable black panthers are melanistic pumas.

The thoughts and opinions expressed by these experts do not provide us with an absolute solution to the black panther mystery, but they do give us a good look into the mindset of zoologists, biologists, and other scientists when it comes to the topic. It would seem all wildlife experts are not necessarily closed-minded to the existence of large, black, long-tailed cats; rather, they simply believe there is no need to assume there is an unknown species out there on which the sightings are based.

15

What to Make of It All

We have covered a lot of ground in the previous chapters. We have established that tales of black panthers are nothing new, and that sightings go back to at least the 1800s and likely further when Native American beliefs and folklore are added to the mix. We have also established that accounts of large, black, long-tailed cats have never really gone away, but instead continue to be reported to the present day. And we have addressed the question of whether or not there is enough suitable habitat for a species of big cat to survive. The locations of sightings have been carefully charted and broken down by region and county. The merits of five suspects – the jaguar, mountain lion, jaguarundi, large domestic/ferals, and escaped exotics - in the sightings of these mysterious cats have been examined. The genetic component behind melanism and the possibility of hybridization has been touched upon, and photographs have been shared and discussed. The scant physical evidence available has been examined, and the opinion of big cat experts sought and received. After all of that, what are we to make of the black panther phenomenon?

When I started this project, I had no idea where it might ultimately lead. I admit to having had some preconceived notions as to what might be at the root of these sightings, but as stated in the introduction, I made a vow to myself to go wherever the evidence might lead. I think I have done that. Some of my preconceived notions have been validated, while I have changed my mind with regards to others. I will attempt to break down my conclusions in the order in which each topic was addressed in this book. The opinions that follow are mine and mine alone. They are based on the research I have done, the interviews and witness statements

I have collected, the thoughts of well-respected wildlife and big cat experts, and the collection of data on sighting locations.

One of the first things I did when I started this project was to look at historical accounts. If these cats were real, I posited, then they did not just show up recently. Early Americans must have had experiences with them. Once I started looking, I did find some interesting reports. I followed up on as many historical accounts as I could and had to decide how much stock to put in them; after all, folklore is a notoriously tough nut to crack when it comes to trying to glean what is fact from what is embellishment and yarn-spinning. I came away not really knowing what to think in some cases but found myself convinced that in others some sort of encounter with a large black, or very dark, cat did take place. If nothing else, what became clear is that the people of times gone by knew what a black panther was and did not regard it as anything extraordinarily rare.

References to these cats in the newspapers and books of the time also provided a solid foundation that people had seen a living and breathing animal. The subtle differences in terminology used by reporters in the mid-to late 1800s and into the early 1900s to identify what species of cat was involved in a particular incident really caught my attention as well. This is most clearly seen in an article from the January 8, 1900, edition of the *San Antonio Daily Light*, featured in Chapter 1, where the reporter speculates on the identity of the wild beast that is to blame for the death of a cow belonging to a local. The writer mentioned that a wildcat, panther, or Mexican lion was likely the culprit – three different terms describing three different species of cat.[199] If this reporter was not differentiating between three different types of cats, he was shockingly redundant in his writing. I do not believe that to be the case, however, and think that the writer knew exactly what he was doing when he used those terms; his readers knew these different cats by the different names he used. This implies familiarity.

I needed no convincing that black panthers were still being seen by Texans and other southerners on a regular basis. I published my first blog post on the topic in August of 2009. I was quickly inundated with emails from readers detailing their own sightings and experiences with large black cats. I was not surprised to hear from fellow Texans on the topic, as they, like I, had grown up believing these phantom cats to be just another animal that inhabited the woods, bottoms, bayous, and swamps of the eastern part of the Lone Star State. I was surprised, shocked even, as to how the reports continued to roll in day after day and week after week. While the pace has slowed somewhat – I am guessing this is due to the fact that the back log of never-before-reported sightings has been pared down significantly over time – it has never stopped. It has been clear to me for some time that people are still seeing something out there that matches the traditional description of a black panther.

Another question that needed to be answered to my satisfaction was simply this: is there enough suitable habitat left in the continental United States, particularly in the southern U.S., to support a breeding population of any kind of big cat? In my opinion, the information shared in Chapter 4 proves there is more than enough room to support at least a small population of puma-sized cats in this country with the American South being a particularly rich environment. The fact that there is room in the South and that there are enough food and water resources available does not mean that these phantom cats exist and are present; however, it does make their existence possible. The South has 265.4 million acres of forest land. That number, for the most part, does not include unpopulated prairies or riparian areas bordering rivers; neither does it include heavily forested and/or undeveloped land that is privately owned. I have been convinced that there are enough wild places with enough resources left in the American South to support a population of big cats.

In microcosm, the spread of mountain lions from what has often been thought of as their last stronghold in the American South - in far western and southern Texas eastward into the Hill Country of Central Texas - proves a population of panther-sized cats can, indeed, survive and thrive in the habitat present. From a macro perspective, mountain lions seem to be trickling back into their former range east of the Mississippi as well. Wildlife officials have been understandably hesitant to publicly state that cougars are back, but the anecdotal evidence is starting to become overwhelming that at least a small number of mountain lions have returned to reclaim their eastern territories. If the mountain lion can survive in the current environment found in the American South, why not another similarly-sized cat?

Once I really started looking at where these sightings were taking place and then charting them, a pattern began to emerge that seemed indicative of a living species. The majority of sightings are clustered in the areas of Texas where a large predatory cat would be most likely to find prey, water, and cover. The correlation between the charted sighting locations and annual average rainfall and other water resources cemented in my mind that people are seeing a real animal. If these black cats were simply figments of the collective imagination of my fellow Texans, there would be no rhyme or reason to the sighting locations; they would have been all over the place. That is simply not the case.

This finding is further supported when the sightings by county map is studied. The fact that nearly all the counties from which sightings have originated are contiguous with other counties from which reports have come again alludes to a living animal being behind the encounters. The suggestion that Texans living in the eastern part of the state are more prone to hallucinate, misidentify known animals, or hoax sighting reports than those living farther to the west is patently ridiculous. I believe the data supplied by the charting of sighting locations points directly at the existence of a real animal.

The basics behind melanism and how it works in the known big cats was touched upon in Chapter 11, albeit in an extremely rudimentary way. It is known that melanism occurs with some regularity in jaguars and leopards, two of our prime suspects in this mystery. Of these two species of big cat, only in the jaguar is the allele for melanism dominant. This could be a significant factor in deciphering the most likely candidate in the black panther conundrum. After working through the various genetic combinations with potential jaguar couplings, it is easy to see how a small population carrying the dominant allele for melanism – if cut off from a larger, more genetically diverse population of jaguars – could produce black offspring almost exclusively. Even if this scenario has not taken place – if natural selection, for whatever reason, has deemed melanism an advantage, as in the leopards of the Malaysian Peninsula – it is possible that black offspring have become the norm. The genetic component is something that must be weighted heavily in any consideration as to what species of cat might be behind the sightings of black panthers.

Also discussed, though not in as much detail, was the possibility that the black panthers of Texas and the American South are hybrid offspring of two different cat species; a coupling between a jaguar and cougar or domestic/feral and a bobcat being the two most commonly discussed theories. It is my opinion that hybridization might explain some individual sightings, especially of cats in the 40-60 lb. range, but it is an unlikely answer for the phenomenon as a whole. To be sure, there are examples in nature of very successful hybrids, but in the animal kingdom, the odds are very much against such couplings occurring often enough to produce a viable new species.

While few in number, there are some intriguing photographs that have been captured over the years of alleged black panthers. Interestingly, they seem to show a wide range of body types and sizes of cat. Some images appear to show animals with features very much like those of a common domestic/feral, while others depict felids that are obviously built similarly to a classic big cat. These discrepancies have led some to simply dismiss the photographic evidence outright. I feel this is a mistake, and the discrepancies in appearance from one cat to another may actually be a very valuable clue: a clue that bolsters my theory on the animal behind this mystery. More on that shortly.

There is one area that has caused me great frustration during my work on this book, and that deals with physical evidence. The nature of my frustration is simple: there is very little physical evidence, and what evidence does exist is simply being ignored or dismissed by wildlife experts. Take the hair samples discussed at length in Chapter 13, for example. These samples were collected from the front bumper of a car belonging to a gentleman from the Dallas area who claims to have hit a large, black, long-tailed cat while traveling a dark highway in central

Texas. He sent me the hairs in the hopes that I could have someone analyze them and find out exactly what type of animal he hit that night. My efforts, however, have been fruitless.

I have not been able to find one single expert in the field who is willing to even look at the hairs under a microscope, much less do any DNA testing. I have been told I am wasting my time, as there has never been any evidence that suggests black panthers are real. When I rebut with the fact that I might have this missing evidence in my possession, I am told my evidence must be fraudulent, as there is no such thing as a black panther. The circuitous nature of these arguments is absolutely infuriating. I do not claim to know from what type of animal the hair samples in my possession came and realize that there is not supposed to be any such creature in North America. I just want to know what is going on out there, and in this case, what animal was struck on that dark Texas State Highway in January of 2013. It has become clear that if there is a resolution to this mystery, amateur naturalists and citizen scientists are going to have to be the ones to truly go after it.

I was fortunate enough to have six highly qualified experts respond to a big cat questionnaire I sent out to them. I am grateful and humbled that they took the time to thoughtfully reply to what was a pretty lengthy series of questions. To recap, none of the experts surveyed believed that an undocumented species of big cat roaming the wilder portions of Texas and the southern United States was responsible for sightings of large, black, long-tailed cats. In that regard, they are very much in the "there is no such thing as a black panther" camp.

But the experts diverged a bit in their thoughts on what might be behind the black panther myth. In particular, I was very intrigued to find out that two of the experts surveyed have had sightings themselves. Lisa Werner of Tiger Creek Wildlife Refuge flatly stated that she and her husband had spotted what they believe was a melanistic jaguar a few years back. Jim Broaddus of Florida's Bear Creek Feline Center is adamant that he once saw a black puma, saying, "I know it was a puma as I train them, work with them, and exhibit them. I know what a puma looks like." The other experts mentioned cases of mistaken identity, tricks of light and perspective, the offspring of hybrid couplings, jaguarundis, and, in rare cases, escaped exotics as potential explanations. As there was no true consensus, some might feel this survey only muddied the black panther waters and feel more confused than ever. But I do not feel that way. I think we are closer than ever to getting to the bottom of things.

Now we come to the million-dollar question: what animal is behind the black panther sightings in Texas and the American South? The merits of each of the five most likely suspects – jaguar, mountain lion, jaguarundi, larger than normal feral cats, and escaped exotic pets – were discussed in Chapters 6-10. There is little doubt in my mind that each of these candidates has accounted for at least a few sightings.

While researching and writing this book, my views have evolved and changed regarding some of these candidates. For example, I used to openly scoff at the notion that a significant number of sightings could be attributable to escaped exotic pets. After looking at the numbers of big cats being kept in this country and just how easy they are to purchase, I am not nearly as adamant in my thinking that escaped or released pets could not be behind more sightings of black panthers in Texas and the American South than I would have believed previously. I was also skeptical that melanistic jaguars could be behind the sightings. While jaguars do exhibit melanism, I reasoned that at most it occurs in only 10% - and that is likely high – of these big cats. If jaguars are behind the sightings, where are the visuals of what should, in my mind, be the more numerous commonly marked animals? Upon discovering that the allele for melanism is dominant in jaguars, however, I have had to reconsider the probability that the largest cat in the New World might be a better candidate than I had thought.

So what is the answer? The most likely explanation for black panther sightings is – and likely always will be – cases of mistaken identity. I have received more than 300 reports from witnesses claiming to have caught a glimpse of one of these big black cats. I have published and charted fewer than half of these reports. The majority of reports were not charted because I felt that the witness was likely mistaken and saw

What to Make of It All 173

some kind of common animal. To be clear, with only a couple of exceptions, I do not feel that witnesses were being less than truthful in their accounts. To the contrary, I believe they did each see an animal of some kind. The knowledge of wildlife varies greatly from person to person, however, and that factor along with others like low-light conditions, exceedingly fleet glimpses of an animal in motion, distance from the subject, etc., all play roles in whether or not I decide to chart a sighting. That being the case, it is all but inarguable that most sightings of black panthers are, indeed, cases of mistaken identity.

But that still leaves a very large body of sightings that I have deemed as most likely genuine. These include cases where the witness got a really good look at the animal; where the witness was very familiar with native wildlife; situations where multiple witnesses were involved; or scenarios where a witness was able to provide minute details that rang true. What of these accounts? What animal is most likely responsible for these sightings? In my mind, there is no one type of animal responsible. I feel strongly that sightings are the result of a combination of seeing several different types of cats.

Many sightings are of animals in the 40-60 lb. range. While it is possible witnesses caught a glimpse of a juvenile cat, it is more likely that they saw a large domestic/feral, jaguarundi, or even, as wildlife expert Jeff Stewart alluded to, the hybrid offspring of a domestic/feral and a bobcat. Anecdotal evidence from around the globe suggests that in some regions, feral cats are growing to larger than normal sizes. I feel the evidence of this occurring in Australia is very strong and see no reason why it could not also happen here in the United States. Most people are simply not prepared to see a cat outside of normal size ranges. If these glimpses are fleeting, as most are, then the witness is going to think panther.

There is anecdotal evidence suggesting that the jaguarundi, whether through natural migration or human introduction, has expanded its range in the United States to include not only deep south Texas but the entire Gulf Coast all the way to Florida. If this is the case, sightings of these long-bodied and odd-looking cats, if they are in the dark morph, could account for reports as well. Most people simply are not familiar with the jaguarundi, and should they encounter one would see a long body, a long tail, and a dark color and jump to the panther conclusion. The jaguarundi is not going to reach the 40-60 lb. range mentioned previously, but again, perspective is a tricky thing, and witnesses unfamiliar with this species might be fooled into thinking they are seeing a larger cat at a greater distance.

I am simply not qualified to comment extensively on the hybrid theory. I know it is possible but also know that most of the time such couplings do not produce offspring capable of reproducing at a high level. But nature has shown us that is not always the case. Countless hybridized plant species are doing quite well in the wild, and history has provided us with some successful hybrid species of animals as well, the red wolf and possibly the Florida panther being two such examples. A coupling between a large domestic/feral and a young bobcat would produce offspring with the genetics to both be black and have a long tail. Why such a coupling would occur in the wild and how often is the question with this scenario. In my mind, it seems likelier the bobcat would eat the domestic/feral than mate with it. Still, if such a coupling has occurred, those genetics are now out there blending with the traits of other cats. Who knows what might arise out of such a witch's brew?

Whether an unusually large domestic/feral, jaguarundi, or some kind of hybrid cat, a witness would be hard-pressed to categorize what he/she was seeing if the sighting was short in duration and the visual was of an animal moving quickly. The witness would know only that he/she saw something bigger or of a different build than a typical cat that was black with a long tail. The conclusion in that scenario is going to be panther, more often than not.

That leaves us with the credible sightings of truly large cats of 60-150+ lbs. Our suspect list here is very short, as there are only a few possibilities. The most likely culprit, in my opinion, is the melanistic jaguar. Jaguars are native to Texas and the American South, and the trait of melanism is not only present in them but is dominant over the trait for a rosette-marked coat. Chester Moore made a great point when answering a survey question about the possibility of mountain lions returning to their historical ranges. To paraphrase, he said they have always been here (in the eastern portion of Texas) and never relegated to only far west and south Texas. I believe this may very well apply to jaguars as well, though in fewer numbers than mountain lions.

In my mind, the idea of a remnant population of jaguars being cut off from the larger population of cats in Mexico and Central America is not outlandish at all. If this remnant population had more melanistic individuals than commonly marked individuals, over time said population could have become nearly totally melanistic due to the dominant nature of the alleles at work. Consider, too, the possibility that the growing rate of human encroachment on their territory and hunting pressure might have forced these cats to become almost exclusively nocturnal. If such a scenario occurred, natural selection might have all but eliminated the common rosette-marked coat of these relic jaguars. A situation where natural selection has all but eliminated the spotted coat of leopards inhabiting the Malaysian Peninsula has already taken place. This is all the more remarkable as the allele for melanism in leopards is recessive. How much likelier is such a scenario in a species where the allele for melanism is already dominant as it is in jaguars? I put a lot of stock into the testimony of experts like Lisa Werner who feels strongly that jaguars are here and probably never left. In my mind, melanistic jaguars have to be suspect number one in sightings where the cat seen was truly large.

A close second on my list of the most likely black panther suspects is the cougar. In some ways, the cougar might be an even more likely candidate than the jaguar. Certainly, the species is more common and widespread. I feel strongly that some witnesses reporting sightings of black panthers saw mountain lions in low light or shadow. Some cougars are grey in color, almost charcoal, and do not exhibit the classic tawny-gold coat so familiar to most people. Seeing a cat of this color could certainly make someone think they were seeing an unfamiliar species. Despite the fact that a melanistic cougar has never been scientifically documented, I cannot totally rule out the possibility. I put a lot of stock in Lisa Werner's opinion that she saw a melanistic jaguar; I feel the same way about Jim Broaddus insisting he saw a black puma. There may be experts out there more familiar with cougars (the Florida panther in particular) than Jim Broaddus, but that list would be extremely short. This gentleman knows his pumas. I cannot simply dismiss his testimonial in which he says he absolutely saw a melanistic *Puma concolor*. We also have the historical accounts from Central and South America where other highly qualified wildlife experts claim to have seen, shot, or documented black cougars. What are we to make of the *cougar noire* as described by French naturalist Georges-Louis Leclerc, Comte de Buffon in his *Histoire Naturelle*? This man was the premier naturalist of his day; I do not think he would list the *cougar noire* as a species in his works unless he was firmly convinced that it truly existed. Again, I cannot simply dismiss the opinion of such an accomplished man.

American scientists, too, have shown interest in whether or not the cougar could exhibit a color other than the typical tawny-blonde in the past. Such was the interest in the late nineteenth century that none other than the United States National Museum, now known as the Smithsonian Institution, commissioned a study trying to get to the bottom of the issue. F.W. True, the first head curator at the United States National Museum, made a special study of the color variations of the puma in 1887.[200] Although the anecdotes of the time seemed credible enough to True and his contemporaries that they decided to examine the issue, they found no definitive proof of a dark-colored variation in cougars. We also have the testimony of William Thomson who claims to have shot a cougar that was "glossy black" on its dorsal surfaces; the photo of the unusually dark puma shot in Costa Rica in 1959 by Miguel Ruiz Herrero; and the countless tales of screaming black panthers, many of which have been documented by East Texas newspaper man Archie Fullingim, that have been around for generations in the Big Thicket of Texas. As neither leopards or jaguars "scream like a hysterical, frightened woman," a cougar is the only possible candidate if a large cat was truly responsible for the terrifying sounds. Can the testimonies of all of these people simply be dismissed? I have a very hard time doing so. Mainstream science may have closed the door on the possibility of melanistic cougars, but in my mind, that door, closed though it may be, is not locked.

It is always difficult to find the middle ground between what a witness says he or she saw and what scientists say is possible. Witnesses are always adamant and can get absolutely combative when an investigator questions them closely or informs them that there is no such animal as a black panther. After all, they know what they saw. On the other hand, there are many mainstream scientists who simply ignore anecdotal reports and assume witnesses are lying, mistaken, or were under the influence of a controlled substance of some kind when a sighting took place.

One would think that the sheer volume of reports of these shadow cats would pique the interest of scientists in Texas, but surprisingly it has not. I find this very disappointing. Some of my hope was restored, however, when I read Ms. Rodrigues's final statement on the big cat questionnaire. When asked about the possibility of there being an undocumented big cat in Texas that could be responsible for these sightings, she said, "Science has surprised me enough over the years that I believe anything is possible. However, at this time I don't think it's probable an undocumented species of big cat exists in the United States." Skeptical? Yes. Open-minded? Yes. These are the traits a true scientist is supposed to exhibit. If more scientists, biologists, and zoologists would adopt this stance, we might finally get to the bottom of this mystery.

Some people are going to be disappointed in my conclusion that there is likely not an undocumented species of big cat out there to explain the black panther phenomenon. I would challenge those people to look at the matter a bit differently. In my mind, almost as wondrous and spectacular as the idea that there is a novel species roaming around out there, is the idea that melanistic jaguars might still roam Texas and the American South; or that mountain lions might, on occasion, be black or very dark (unlikely as that might be); or that jaguarundis, thought to be extremely rare and endangered, might actually be more numerous and widespread than previously thought.

I would also like to stress that you can do your part to help solve this mystery. Should you ever find yourself taking a road trip through the backwoods, river bottoms, swamps, or bayous of Texas or the American South, consider yourself as more than just a traveler; think of yourself as a citizen scientist. Be ready. Keep your eyes open and a camera handy. Something is out there, and you just might be the one who brings the black panther out of the realm of myth and into reality.

Now, wouldn't that be something?

Acknowledgements

WRITING THIS BOOK has truly been one of the most difficult, yet rewarding, experiences of my life. I have learned that one does not finish a project like this without a great deal of help. I simply could not have completed it without the cooperation of a great number of people to whom I would like to express my heartfelt gratitude. Thank you for your friendship, patience, expertise, and input. A special thank you to those who have shared photographs.

Among them are Charles Adams, Jim Broaddus, Dr. Angelo Capparella, Kevin Chambers, the City of Ruidoso, New Mexico Public Library, the City of Temple, Texas Public Library, Daryl Colyer, Herman Colyer, Alex Espinoza, Dan Florek, Jim Fowler, David Hansen, Alton Higgins, Gail Kennedy, Angelo Landrum, Travis Lawrence, Mark McClurken, Sandra McGath, Chester Moore, Jr., Tod Pinkerton, William Rebsamen, Matt Rhyner, Amy Rodrigues, Michelle Schireman, Terry "Tex" Tolar, the Townsend Memorial Library of the University of Mary-Hardin Baylor, Baron Victor, Amanda Ward, Lisa Werner, Mike Williams, and, of course, all the witnesses who have submitted reports.

Jeff Stewart, I could have written the book without your input, but the project would have been poorer for it. Thank you for all your help, my friend.

Most of all, I want to thank my wife, Holly; the most understanding and encouraging person I know. I love you.

Sightings Appendix

THIS IS A LIST OF THE CREDIBLE SIGHTINGS of black panthers I have charted in the state of Texas. Each item includes the date the sighting was reported to me—not necessarily the date the encounter took place—and a brief synopsis of the incident. The sightings all occurred between 2010 and 2017 unless otherwise noted. For additional details visit the black panther sightings distribution map at Texascryptidhunter.blogspot.com

Reported 2/24/10: A motorist reports spotting an "enormous cat with a long tail" crossing a busy road in front of his vehicle. The color was "very, very dark brown."

Reported 7/17/10: A man reports seeing a large, sleek, black cat cross a road in front of his vehicle near the old ghost town of Ohio.

Reported 7/31/10: A motorist spots a large "black panther" dart across the road near Arbor Hills Nature Preserve.

Reported 8/22/10: A man reports seeing a large black cat on a bike trail outside of Mineral Wells.

Reported 8/26/10: Multiple witnesses watch a large "black panther" creep, as if stalking prey, across an empty field on the family property. Several people watched the cat through binoculars for up to 30 seconds.

Reported 9/2/10: A pair of witnesses observe a very large black cat through binoculars outside of Quitman.

Reported 10/18/10: An Anderson County resident reports two sightings of a very large "black or very dark brown cat with a long tail" over a multi-year period.

Reported 11/22/10: A man, observing his deer feeder through binoculars from his house, sees a large black cat weighing approximately 50 lbs. with a long tail move out of the woods to the feeder area. The witness was able to observe the cat for about 15 seconds before it returned to the woods.

Reported 11/24/10: A pair of motorists spot a "huge, Great Dane-sized" black cat run across FM 69.

Reported 1/6/11: A former pipeline worker recalls seeing a panther as "black as coal" while clearing a right-of-way in the heart of The Big Thicket National Preserve back in the 1960s.

Reported 1/11/11: Three witnesses see a "3-foot-tall black cat with a long tail" standing just off the access road of I-35W.

Reported 1/22/11: A rural resident reports multiple sightings of a "mastiff-sized black cat with an extremely long tail" on and near his property.

Reported 1/30/11: A man recalls his father (a manager at a chicken farm) telling him of seeing a large black cat near the chicken houses on multiple occasions, usually in the wee hours of the morning.

Reported 3/3/11: Witness reports multiple sightings of a very large gray/charcoal-colored cat with a long tail that was "far too large to be a domestic."

Reported 3/23/11: While checking a hog trap, a man is startled when a large, thick, black cat, estimated at 80-90 lbs., bolts across his path and into the woods.

Reported 8/9/11: A man and wife see a "cougar with a slick, smooth, black coat and big square head" cross the road in front of their vehicle.

Reported 8/9/11: A man reports multiple sightings of a pair of large black cats with cubs near McDade.

Reported 8/9/11: A man and his daughter witness an approximately 5-foot-long, 3-foot-high, black cat emerge from a culvert near a water treatment plant.

Reported 9/1/11: A motorist spots a very dark brown or black cat weighing approximately 60 lbs.

Reported 11/9/11: A hunter reports taking two shots at an "absolutely black cat with a tail as long as its body" outside of Llano but misses.

Reported 11/24/11: A witness watches a large black cat with a long tail running across a field.

Reported 12/3/11: A rancher reports a sighting of a "black panther" on his land outside of Hillsboro.

Reported 12/7/11: A woman sees a "German Shepherd-sized" dark brown/black cat cross the road in front of her vehicle.

Reported 1/5/12: A resident reports seeing a "panther-sized black cat" outside of Fort Worth.

Reported 1/5/12: A *Texas Cryptid Hunter* reader recalls a sighting of two "black panthers" as a youth.

Reported 1/9/12: A witness sees a "solid black mountain lion with a tail as long as its body."

Reported 1/11/12: A driver spies a "black panther" crouched on the side of state Highway 285. It was "as if it was waiting to cross."

Reported 2/15/12: A hunter captures an image of a large black cat on his game camera that was set up at a deer feeder.

Reported 5/16/12: The owner of an RV park reports a large "black panther" that strolled through the campground.

Reported 6/11/12: A family of three spots a "lab-sized black cat with a long tail" stalking a wooded area behind their fence line.

Reported 6/19/12: Resident sees a "large thick cat with fur like black velvet and too big to be a dog" walking in a creek bed that winds through his residential neighborhood.

Reported 7/12/12: A motorist observes a very large black cat cross FM535 outside of Smithville.

Reported 7/16/12: A woman walking her dog near a wooded area close to Klein High School reports being intimidated by a large black cat.

Reported 7/18/12: A hunter prepping for hunting season reports seeing a large black cat on his lease.

Reported 7/27/12: A man recounts childhood encounters with a family of large black cats seen periodically up until at least the mid 1980s.

Reported 2/11/13: A homeowner reports seeing a very large black cat in a green belt in the Great Hills area of Austin.

Reported 2/13/13: A *Texas Cryptid Hunter* reader recounts a childhood sighting of a "black panther" while hunting near Stillhouse Hollow Lake.

Reported 3/10/13: An uncle and his nephew witness a pair of black cats that were "bigger than a cougar" run across a county road and into an abandoned house.

Reported 3/29/13: A witness reports seeing a larger black cat, matching the description of a jaguarundi, in Burnet County.

Reported 4/20/13: A property owner reports a face-to-face encounter with a "black panther" that was an estimated 5 feet long and 80-100 lbs. while out tending to her horses.

Reported 5/23/13: A motorist spots a large black cat with a long tail crossing the road in front of his vehicle. The larger cat was quickly followed by three small cubs of the same color walking in single file order.

Reported 6/6/13: A hiker reports walking up on a large black cat that looked like "something between a jaguar and a mountain lion."

Reported 6/8/13: A rancher reports seeing large, long-tailed cats that are "black in color but with spots visible" 1-2 times a year over a 20-year period.

Reported 6/12/13: A motorist on the way to work spots a large "deep brown or black" cat matching the description of a jaguarundi dart across the road.

Reported 6/15/13: A motorist reports spotting a "yellow-eyed black cat "nearly the height of a Great Dane" dart across the road in front of his vehicle. The witness claimed that spots were visible even though the cat was black.

Reported 6/19/13: A motorist reports seeing a large black cat cross the road in front of his vehicle around dawn.

Reported 6/19/13: A motorist reports spotting a large "black panther" cross the road in front of him and run toward the Sabinal River bottoms.

Reported 6/24/13: A motorist watches a large black cat, approximately 4 feet long and 75 lbs., cross state Highway 187.

Reported 7/19/13: A hiker sees a "deer-sized" black cat

walking leisurely down a hiking trail.

Reported 7/23/13: A motorist spots a "big black cat the size of a mountain lion" cross state Highway 69 and bound into a pasture.

Reported 8/2/13: A rancher reports seeing "three cougars, two of which were black" over a period of several decades.

Reported 8/8/13: Multiple witnesses see a "huge, 100% black cat with a long tail" eating a chicken near a barn on their property. The cat retreated upon being seen.

Reported 8/13/13: A rancher reports multiple sightings of a long black cat approaching 3 feet in length with a long tail matching the description of a jaguarundi.

Reported 8/16/13: A hunter recalls multiple sightings of large charcoal/deep brown cats during the 2011 and 2012 hunting seasons.

Reported 8/25/13: A motorist sees a large black cat run in front of his car while traveling on the Alamo Parkway.

Reported 9/2/13: A San Felipe resident reports multiple sightings of "black spotted cats," including a female with two cubs, be- tween 1998-2007 along the Brazos River.

Reported 9/28/13: Witness reports a sighting of a "large black cat with a tail as long as its body and bigger than a bobcat."

Reported 10/1/13: A witness reports spotting a 3.5-foot-long black cat with a long tail, flat head, and small upright ears on his property. The description fits that of a jaguarundi.

Reported 10/29/13: A homeowner reports seeing a "massive" black cat with a long tail cross a field adjacent to his property.

Reported 10/31/13: A motorist reports watching a large black cat chase a deer across the road in front of his car.

Reported 11/1/13: A motorist sees a "black panther" running in front of her car on FM 2549.

Reported 11/1/13: A hunter reports seeing a black cat "too big to be a jaguarundi."

Reported 11/17/13: A rural Wise County resident drives up on a large black cat feeding on a freshly killed goat.

Reported 11/17/13: A rancher sees a large black cat with a long tail while out feeding cattle.

Reported 12/1/13: A hunter reports seeing a very dark brown/black cat from his stand from about 300 yards. He watched the cat through his scope for several minutes.

Reported 12/10/13: A witness recalls seeing a 4-foot-long "black panther" nailed to a fence when he was 18 years-old (1984).

Reported 12/25/13: A Hooks resident reports two separate "black panther" sightings over a multi- year period.

Reported 1/6/14: A motorist spots a 2.5-foot-tall black cat dart across the road. The cat had a long tail.

Reported 1/8/14: A longtime hunter relates two sightings of "black panthers" in his 20 years of hunting.

Reported 1/16/14: A hunter recalls being stalked by a "black panther" in 1969.

Reported 1/18/14: A hunter spies a "lab-sized black cat (approximately 80 lbs.) with a shiny black coat and a long tail" on his hunting lease.

Reported 1/29/14: A Tyler, Texas, veterinarian reports seeing a "black panther" cross the road in front of her vehicle.

Reported 1/29/14: A homeowner reports watching a "black panther" attempting to get into a goat pen.

Reported 2/13/14: A *Texas Cryptid Hunter* reader captures a series of photos of a charcoal/black cat of some kind in the Texas Hill Country.

Reported 3/5/14: A man walking his two German Shepherds encounters a dark cat with a long tail weighing approximately 30 lbs. Upon being seen, the cat leaps into a tree and disappears.

Reported 3/17/14: A homeowner watches a "6-foot-long cat with a long tail" walking along a wooded area adjacent to a creek near his property.

Reported 3/24/14: A large black cat "bigger than a bobcat but smaller than a cougar" with a long tail is reported by a motorist.

Reported 3/28/14: A game camera captures a photo of an extremely dark cougar menacing a buck at a deer feeder.

Reported 4/11/14: A motorist reports a "black panther" crossing a road in broad daylight.

Reported 4/12/14: A landowner spots a very large (approximately 100 lbs.) black cat leap a 4-foot-tall fence on his property. He reports the cat exhibited yellow eyeshine.

Reported 4/22/14: A man and his two daughters spot

a large charcoal-colored cat while biking. The witnesses estimated the cat was 2.5 feet high and 4 feet long with small, upright ears.

Reported 5/5/14: A man reports seeing a black cat "too large to have been a bobcat with a long tail like a mountain lion" south of Sierra Blanca.

Reported 5/6/14: A motorist spots a cougar-sized black cat with a long tail bounding through a pasture.

Reported 5/19/14: Two fishermen report having seen a large black cat back in 2010. The pair recall that several calves were killed, and strange screams were heard in the community about that same time.

Reported 6/9/14: A family returns home to find a large "black panther" lying on the roof of a small shed near the back of their property which bordered the Colorado River.

Reported 6/23/14: A motorist spots a large black cat, approximately 5 feet in length, bound across the Sam Houston Tollway.

Reported 6/30/14: A farmer recalls spotting a large "black panther" on his property in the spring of 2013.

Reported 7/8/14: A husband and wife have separate sightings of a very large "dark brown or black" cat with a long tail in a field behind their apartment.

Reported 7/25/14: A man encounters a "black panther" while horseback riding. The horse was spooked by the big cat and bolted.

Reported 7/26/14: A large black cat is photographed near a construction site of the west side of Lake Ray Hubbard.

Reported 8/1/14: A soldier reports two separate sightings of long-tailed black cats in the wilderness/training areas of Fort Hood.

Reported 8/9/14: Hunter finds a deer carcass cached in a tree. He spots a large black cat in the same area three weeks later.

Reported 8/10/14: Cyclist spots a large black cat with a long tail. The witness estimated the weight of the cat at 50 lbs. The cat jumped an 8-foot-tall fence and escaped view.

Reported 8/11/14: A pair of senior citizens spot a large black cat lounging on a golf course green while out on an evening stroll.

Reported 8/29/14: A Texas Silica employee reports multiple sightings of "black panthers" near the small lakes on the company's property over a period of several months.

Reported 9/1/14: A farmer reports spotting a large black cat with a long tail that was "much bigger than a bobcat" on his property.

Reported 9/8/14: A homeowner reports seeing a 3-to-4-foot-long cat with a long tail. The cat was very dark with "spots visible" on the coat.

Reported 9/17/14: Two hunters spot a "black panther" trailing a deer.

Reported 10/6/14: Three adults and one child all witness a "panther," approximately 4 feet long and estimated to weigh in the 80-lb. range, dart across traffic near the Barton Creek Green Belt.

Reported 10/10/14: A Mineral Wells resident spots a "black panther" while out on a walk.

Reported 10/13/14: Homeowner reports seeing a "black panther" cross a pasture after hearing his cows bawling in fear. He added that there were reports of missing pets and livestock in the area in the days preceding and immediately after his sighting.

Reported 9/29/15: A witness reports a frightening close

encounter with a large black cat with a long tail outside of Dayton.

Reported 9/30/15: A motorist reports a daytime sighting of a "very dark cougar" crossing FM 723 south of Katy. The witness estimated the cat weighed 75-100 lbs.

Reported 10/18/15: A motorist spots a large black cat with "yellow eyes" in the tall grass of state Highway 21 east of Alto.

Reported 11/7/15: A motorist spots a "cougar-shaped" black cat (smaller than a mountain lion but shaped like one) as it crosses the road in front of him outside of Nocona.

Reported 11/24/15: A witness spots a very large black cat sauntering across her property from her kitchen window. The home is near the San Bernard River.

Reported 12/2/15: A motorist spots a 25-35 lb. black cat chasing a low-flying bird across Lake Shore Drive near the Bosque River on the outskirts of Waco.

Reported 12/7/15: Huge, dark brown cat with thick, long tail reported along FM 1509.

Reported 12/9/15: Large, "coal black" cat sighted in broad daylight by a hiker and his daughter.

Sightings Appendix *195*

Reported 12/22/15: Large, otter-like, black cat sighted by land owner while driving his tractor. Likely a jaguarundi.

Reported 1/21/16: A witness encounters a large black cat and a cub while walking home from a relative's house on a rural road.

Reported 1/29/16: A witness spots a cat matching the textbook description of a charcoal-colored jaguarundi in a field behind his home.

Reported 2/4/16: A witness reports seeing a "very, very dark cougar" while fishing a private stock pond outside of Wills Point.

Reported 2/5/16: Two hikers have a nighttime encounter with a large black cat while walking their dog at the Arbor Hills Nature Preserve.

Reported 2/10/16: A motorist sees a black cat with a long tail "bigger than a pit bull" cross FM 1243.

Reported 2/21/16: A pair of hikers and their dog are frightened by a very large black cat with a long tail that crossed the trail within 150-feet of them.

Reported 2/23/16: A hunter watches a "black panther" chase a bobcat up a tree.

Reported 2/23/16: A motorist witnesses a "black panther" narrowly escape being hit by an oncoming vehicle outside of Queen City as it crossed FM 74.

Reported 2/26/16: A witness recalls watching a large "black cougar or panther" cross the road in front of his vehicle back in 1986.

Reported 3/20/16: A gate guard reports seeing a 4-foot-long black cat with a "huge tail" come out from under a bus and snatch up a dead rat.

Reported 4/9/16: A witness reports multiple sightings of a "big brown cougar" and a "black jaguar-sized cat" outside of Emory.

Reported 5/20/16: A woman reports encountering a "husky- sized" black cat while walking her dogs in a subdivision that backs up to un- developed land.

Reported 5/23/16: A man reports watching a "very large black cat" running through his pasture at approximately 2:00 p.m. in broad daylight.

Reported 5/23/16: A camper and her daughter spot a large black cat with "green eyes" on a walking trail just before dusk. The witness reports that park personnel "ridiculed" her when she told them what she saw.

Reported 5/26/16: A rancher reports seeing a large dark cat with "yellow eyes" walking up his driveway.

Reported 7/24/16: A mother and daughter recall seeing a large "black panther with huge feet" sauntering across the road in the summer of 2010 or 2011.

Reported 7/26/16: A witness reports seeing a "weird-looking," dark-colored cat with a long tail, long body, and flat head run across the road in front of him just before dusk.

Reported 7/31/16: A property owner reports the sighting of a large black cat and the location of a possible den site after moving on to a piece of rural property that had been unoccupied for the last 30-40 years.

Reported 8/1/16: A witness reports multiple sightings of a "black panther" during the 1970s on family property near Flat Fork Creek outside of Tenaha.

Reported 9/4/16: A motorist spots a "very large but thin and lanky black cat" crossing a road. The witness felt the head did not fit the description of a jaguarundi and it was too big to be that species despite its gaunt appearance.

Reported 9/22/16: Motorist reports seeing a "massive black cat" in his driveway upon his return home at approximately 10:45 p.m. The witness estimates the cat's weight at somewhere between 120-150 lbs.

Reported 11/18/16: A man reports a close-up (25 yards) encounter with a "mountain lion-sized black cat" while out walking his dog.

Reported 2/17/17: A family reports multiple sightings of black cats "bigger than their 60 lb. dog." Sightings included cats walking the fence line of the property and road crossings.

Reported 2/21/17: A motorist spots a very large black cat drinking from a small pond. The cat ran and jumped into a large oak tree when the witness slowed down to get a better look.

Reported 2/28/17: Witness spots a "Great Dane-sized black cat with marbled coat" just beyond a small rock wall at the back of his home.

Reported 4/2/17: A man recalls seeing a "black panther" trailing a doe while hunting as a boy.

Reported 4/2/17: A man recalls watching a "Momma black panther and two cubs" cross a pipeline right of way he was clearing through the piney woods outside of Livingston. The cats were seen multiple times by several people during the course of the project.

Reported 4/14/17: A resident reports seeing a large black cat with a long tail walking the fence line of his property outside of Mount Calm.

Reported 4/17/17: Three men recall seeing a "cougar-sized jet black Cat" lying on the hood of a car upon exiting their home on a very cold Saturday morning back in 2011.

Reported 4/25/17: Witness reports periodic jaguarundi sightings over a period of several years.

Reported 5/11/17: A man recalls spotting a "black panther" while horseback riding on an old logging road between Willow Creek and Spring Creek in southeast Texas back in (approximately) 1966.

Reported 5/11/17: A witness reports encountering an approximately 150-lb. black cat in his driveway when he went to check on his barking dogs. He estimated the cat was 5 feet long and approached 3 feet in height at the shoulder.

Reported 5/11/17: Two women on their way to a college football game spot a large black cat crossing the road in front of their car. The witnesses were "shocked by the size" of the cat.

Reported 5/15/17: A motorist watches a "black panther the size of a large dog" cross the road in front of his vehicle. The witness said he had a good look as the cat seemed to be in no hurry to cross.

Reported 6/5/17: Resident reports multiple sightings of large black cats (too big to be jaguarundis) on and near her property.

Reported 6/7/17: A member of a survey crew stumbles upon a sleeping "German shepherd-sized" black cat in a brushy area near his work site.

Reported 7/25/17: Saginaw resident photographs a large black cat pacing her fence line.

Reported 7/29/17: Resident spots an approximately 70-lb. cat, very dark, with "yellow eyes and a black coat that looked like it might have been a little sun-bleached."

References and Citations

Chapter 1

1. Lewis, Chad, and Nick Redfern. *Hidden headlines of Texas: strange, unusual, & bizarre newspaper stories 1860-1910.* Eau Claire, WI: Unexplained Research Pub. Co., 2007. Print. Page 52.
2. Ibid., 64.
3. *World War II Divisional Combat Chronicles.* N.p., n.d. Web. 19 June 2017.
4. "History of 66th." *66th Division.* N.p., n.d. Web. 19 June 2017.

Chapter 2

5. Personal conversation with the author.
6. "Native American Panther Mythology." *Native American Indian Panther Legends, Meaning and Symbolism from the Myths of Many Tribes.* N.p., n.d. Web. 16 June 2017.
7. "Aztec Warriors." *Ancient Aztec Warriors.* N.p., n.d. Web. 16 June 2017.
8. Martin, Howard N. *Myths & folktales of the Alabama-Coushatta Indians of Texas.* Austin, TX: Encino Press, 1977. Print.
9. "The Black Panthers of the Louisiana-Texas Borderlands: Are They Extinct?" *Black Panthers.* N.p., n.d. Web. 16 June 2017.
10. Ibid..
11. Ibid.
12. Ibid.

13 Ibid.
14 Ibid.
15 Eason, I. C., and Blair Pittman. *The stories of I.C. Eason, King of the Dog People*. Denton, TX: U of North Texas Press, 1996. Print. Pages 30-32.
16 Dobie, J. Frank, and Barbara Latham. *Tales of old-time Texas*. Boston: Little, Brown and Company, 1955. Print. Pages 187-188.
17 "From the woods of Montgomery County, AR." *Panther in Montgomery Co. Arkansas*. N.p., n.d. Web. 16 June 2017.
18 Shuker, Dr Karl. "An American Mystery Black Panther Depicted in a Famous Modern-Day Painting." *ShukerNature*. N.p., 15 Apr. 2016. Web. 06 July 2017.

Chapter 3

19 Personal conversation with the author.
20 Stienstra, Tom. "Bear, black lion - impossible? Not necessarily." *SFGate*. N.p., 09 Aug. 2009. Web. 19 June 2017.
21 Ibid.
22 From the notes of Dr. Angelo Caparrella.
23 Ibid.
24 Ibid.
25 Gerhard, Ken. *Monsters of Texas*. N.p.: Great Britain by CFZ Press, 2010. Print. Page 112.
26 Ibid..
27 Personal correspondence (email) with the author.
28 Personal correspondence (FB IM) with the author.
29 Personal correspondence (email) with the author.

Chapter 4

30 "U.S. Forest Facts and Historical Trends." U.S. Department of Agriculture, n.d. Web. 19 June 2017. Page 3.

31 "Alabama Forest Facts." *Forest Facts*. Alabama Forestry Commission, n.d. Web. 19 June 2017.

32 "Arkansas Forestry Facts." *Forestry*. Laurie W. Warren, n.d. Web. 19 June 2017.

33 "Florida Forestry." *Florida Forestry Association*. N.p., n.d. Web. 19 June 2017.

34 Hoyle, Zoe. "Georgia Forests 2011." *Georgia Forests, 2011 | News and Events | SRS*. U.S. Forest Service, 26 July 2012. Web. 19 June 2017.

35 Communications, Zoe Hoyle SRS Science. "Latest Forest Inventory for Kentucky." *CompassLive*. U.S. Forest Service, 11 Sept. 2012. Web. 19 June 2017.

36 "2014 Louisiana Forestry Facts." *Lousianaforestry.com*. Louisiana Forestry Association, n.d. Web. 19 June 2017.

37 "Forestry in Mississippi." *Farm Families of Mississippi*. N.p., n.d. Web. 19 June 2017.

38 "NC Forest Data." *North Carolina Forestry Association*. N.p., n.d. Web. 19 June 2017.

39 "Oklahoma's Forests." *Oklahoma Forestry Services*. N.p., n.d. Web. 19 June 2017.

40 "State of SC's Forests by the Numbers 2015." *South Carolina Forestry Commission*. N.p., n.d. Web. 19 June 2017.

41 "Texas Almanac - The Source for All Things Texan Since 1857." *Forest Resources | Texas Almanac*. N.p., n.d. Web. 19 June 2017.

42 "Forests." *Forests - TN.Gov*. N.p., n.d. Web. 19 June 2017.

43 "Facts About Virginia Forests." *Forested Acreage, Ownership, and Tree Inventory Data | Virginia Department of Forestry |*. Virginia Department of Forestry, n.d. Web. 19 June 2017.

44 "U.S. Forest Resource Facts and Historical Trends." *U.S. Forest Ser-*

vice. Ed. Sonja N. Oswalt and W. Brad Smith. N.p., Aug. 2014. Web.

45 *Forest Facts, Alaska Forest Association*. N.p., n.d. Web. 19 June 2017.

46 Colyer, Daryl, and Alton Higgins. "Wood Ape Sightings: Correlations to Annual Rainfall Totals, Waterways, Human Population Densities and Black Bear Habitat Zones." http://www.woodape.org. N.p., n.d. Web. 19 June 2017.

47 Griego, Monique. "Mountain Lion Shot and Killed in Downtown El Paso." *Fox News*. FOX News Network, 11 May 2011. Web. 19 June 2017.

48 Abramovitch, Seth. "Mountain Lion Killed After Wandering Into Downtown Santa Monica (Video)." *The Hollywood Reporter*. N.p., 22 May 2012. Web. 19 June 2017.

49 Fleischer, Tim. "Mountain lion kill spotted in downtown Salado." *Salado Village Voice*. N.p., 01 Mar. 2017. Web. 19 June 2017.

50 Morrison, Dan. "Cougar Shot in Chicago; Was 1,000 Miles From Home?" *National Geographic*. National Geographic Society, 17 Apr. 2008. Web. 19 June 2017.

51 Chiland, Elijah. "LA area mountain lions are surprisingly urban." *Curbed LA*. Curbed LA, 14 July 2016. Web. 19 June 2017.

52 "Next-door leopards: First GPS-collar study reveals how leopards live with people." *ScienceDaily*. Wildlife Conservation Society, 21 Nov. 2014. Web. 19 June 2017.

Chapter 5

53 Mayes, Michael C. "Black Panther Distribution Map." *Google Maps*. Texas Cryptid Hunter, 8 Feb. 2016. Web. 21 June 2017.

Chapter 6

54 "How Recently did the Jaguar (*Panthera onca*) Roam Eastern North America?" *GeorgiaBeforePeople*. N.p., 26 Sept. 2012. Web. 21 June 2017.

55 Ibid.
56 Wood, W. Raymond. "The Jaguar Gorget—"The Missouri State Artifact"." *Museum of Anthropology, College of Arts and Science, University of Missouri*. Missouri Archaeological Society Quarterly, Apr. 2000. Web. 21 June 2017.
57 Lawson, John. N.p.: n.p., n.d. *Gutenberg.org*. Project Gutenberg, July 1999. Web. 21 June 2017.
58 Ibid.
59 "How Recently did the Jaguar (*Panthera onca*) Roam Eastern North America?" *Georgia Before People*. N.p., 26 Sept. 2012. Web. 21 June 2017.
60 *Was the Black Panther Actually a Jaguar?* N.p., n.d. Web. 21 June 2017.
61 Ibid.
62 Dobie, J. Frank, Mody C. Boatright, and Harry Huntt Ranson, eds. *Mustangs and cow horses*. Denton, TX: U of North Texas Press, 2000. Print. Pages 30-31.
63 *Was the Black Panther Actually a Jaguar?* N.p., n.d. Web. 21 June 2017.
64 Sinclair, Steve. "The Last Jaguar." *Valley Morning Star*. N.p., 21 June 2008. Web. 21 June 2017.
65 Rosatte, Rick. "Evidence Confirms the Presence of Cougars (*Puma concolor*) in Ontario, Canada." *Eastern Cougar*. Ontario Ministry of Natural Resources, 2011. Web.
66 Ibid.
67 Personal conversation with the author.
68 Ibid.
69 Weidensaul, Scott. N.p.: n.p., n.d. *Return to Wild America: A Yearlong Search for the Continent's Natural Soul*. Farrar, Straus and Giroux, 2006. Web. 21 June 2017.
70 Pappas, Stephanie. "Arizona's Only Jaguar Prowls a Difficult, But Hopeful, Path." *LiveScience*. N.p., 03 Mar. 2016. Web. 21 June 2017.
71 Tony Davis Arizona Daily. "US seeks to shield jaguar habitat." *Arizona Daily Star*. N.p., 18 Aug. 2012. Web. 21 June 2017.

Chapter 7

72 "Mountain Lion (*Puma concolor*)." *RSS*. Texas Parks & Wildlife, n.d. Web. 21 June 2017.

73 "Basic Facts About Mountain Lions." *Defenders of Wildlife*. N.p., 19 Sept. 2016. Web. 21 June 2017.

74 *ITIS Standard Report Page: Puma concolor*. N.p., n.d. Web. 21 June 2017.

75 "Frequently Asked Questions About Mountain Lions." *Mountain Lion Foundation*. N.p., n.d. Web. 21 June 2017.

76 Wilder, Laura Ingalls. *Little House in the Big Woods*. New York, NY: HarperCollins, 1953. Print.

77 "Welcome to C.A.R.E." *CARE*. N.p., n.d. Web. 21 June 2017.

78 Abernethy, Francis Edward. *Tales from the Big Thicket*. Austin: U of Texas Press, 1966. Print. Pages 22-25.

79 Ibid.

80 Ibid.

81 Buffon, G. 1772-1809. Naturgeschichte der Vogel. 35 *volumes*. Volumes 1-6 translated by F. H. Martini and volumes 7-35 translated by B. C. Otto. Pauli, Berlin.

82 Shuker, Dr Karl. "The Truth About Black Pumas - Separating Fact From Fiction Regarding Melanistic Cougars." *ShukerNature*. N.p., 16 Aug. 2012. Web. 21 June 2017.

83 Ibid..

84 Stewart, Keff. "Cryptid Cats." *PhilosoPhenomena* Unity Fest. Glen Rose, TX. 25 Nov. 2016. Lecture.

85 Witherspoon, Tommy. "Black cougar sightings have Waco neighborhood on alert." *Waco Tribune-Herald,* WacoTrib.com. N.p., 01 Mar. 2013. Web. 21 June 2017.

86 Ibid.

87 Ibid.

88 Ibid.

Chapter 8

89 "Jaguarundi videos, photos and facts." *Arkive*. N.p., n.d. Web. 21 June 2017.
90 *Big Cat Rescue*. N.p., n.d. Web. 21 June 2017.
91 Rick, Jessica. "Puma yagouaroundi (jaguarundi)." *Animal Diversity Web*. N.p., 2004. Web. 21 June 2017.
92 Ibid.
93 Oliveira, Tadeu G. "Herpailurus yagouaroundi." *Mammalian Species* 578 (1998): 1-6. Web. 21 June 2017.
94 Wojcik, Lisa. "Florida Jaguarundi Report." *Pangea Institute*. N.p., Aug. 2006. Web. 21 June 2017.
95 "Alpheus Hyatt Verrill." *Wikipedia*. Wikimedia Foundation, n.d. Web. 21 June 2017.
96 "Strange, weird animal found on property of upstate man." *Mobile Register,* 25 Jan. 1975: n. pag. Print.

Chapter 9

97 Mott, Maryann. "U.S. Faces Growing Feral Cat Problem." *National Geographic*. National Geographic Society, 7 Sept. 2004. Web. 21 June 2017.
98 Ibid.
99 Ibid.
100 Lever, Christopher. *Naturalized animals: the ecology of successfully introduced species*. London: Poyser, 1994. Print.
101 Loss, Scott R., Tom Will, and Peter P. Marra. 2013. The Impact of Free-ranging Domestic Cats on Wildlife of the United States. Nature Communications 4, article #1396.

102 Williams, Michael, and Rebecca Lang. *Australian big cats: an unnatural history of panthers*. Hazelbrook, N.S.W.: Strange Nation Publishing, 2010. Print. Page 285

103 Wahlquist, Calla. "Feral cats now cover 99.8% of Australia." *The Guardian*. Guardian News and Media, 04 Jan. 2017. Web. 21 June 2017.

104 Fleming, Atticus. "Saving Australia's Threatened Wildlife." *Australian Wildlife Conservancy*. N.p., 2012. Web. 21 June 2017.

105 Williams, Michael, and Rebecca Lang. *Australian big cats: an unnatural history of panthers*. Hazelbrook, N.S.W.: Strange Nation Publishing, 2010. Print. Pages 64-67.

106 Ibid., 65

107 Ibid., 67-68

108 Ibid., 151-152

109 Ibid., 111-117

110 Ibid., 117

111 Drive, ABC Statewide, and Supplied. "Big cats in Victoria: DSE study says they're just feral but case not closed." *ABC Ballarat - Australian Broadcasting Corporation*. N.p., 18 Sept. 2012. Web. 21 June 2017.

112 Williams, Michael, and Rebecca Lang. *Australian big cats: an unnatural history of panthers*. Hazelbrook, N.S.W.: Strange Nation Publishing, 2010. Print. Page 286

113 Ibid.

114 Ibid.

115 Ibid.

Chapter 10

116 "Facts about the Exotic Pet Trade." *Animal Planet*. N.p., 01 Oct. 2014. Web. 22 June 2017.

117 Hessler, Katherine, and Tanith Balaban. "Exotic Animals as

Pets." *American Bar Association*. Americanbar.org. N.p., July 2009. Web. 22 June 2017.

118 "Facts about the Exotic Pet Trade." *Animal Planet*. N.p., 01 Oct. 2014. Web. 22 June 2017.

119 "More Tigers in American Backyards than in the Wild." *WWF*. World Wildlife Fund, 29 July 2014. Web. 22 June 2017.

120 "Fast Facts: Burmese Pythons in Florida." *FAQs: Burmese Pythons in Florida*. N.p., n.d. Web. 22 June 2017.

121 Walsh, Bryan. "Burmese Pythons Are Taking Over the Everglades." *Time*. Time.com, 20 May 2015. Web. 22 June 2017.

122 Hallmark, Bob. "Piranha sub-species caught in East Texas lake." *KLTV.com - Channel 7 News, Weather, & Sports for East Texas - KLTV.com - Tyler, Longview, Jacksonville*. N.p., 15 Mar. 2012. Web. 22 June 2017.

123 Price, Bob. "Deadly Cobra Holds Texas Cops at Bay." *Breitbart*. Breitbart.com. N.p., 30 July 2015. Web. 22 June 2017.

124 "Argentine black and white tegu." *Nonnative Reptiles*. N.p., n.d. Web. 22 June 2017.

125 "Invasive Lionfish." *Invasive Lionfish | Flower Garden Banks National Marine Sanctuary*. N.p., n.d. Web. 22 June 2017.

126 Michael Kruse. "Nile monitor lizards invaded Florida and they're winning the battle." *Tampa Bay Times*. N.p., 19 June 2009. Web. 22 June 2017.

127 BCR. "How Much Is That 'Kitty' In the Window?" *Big Cat Rescue*. N.p., 12 Mar. 2017. Web. 22 June 2017.

128 Ibid.

129 Ibid.

130 "Summary of State Laws Relating to the Private Possession of Exotic Animals." *Born Free* . N.p., Oct. 2016. Web. 22 June 2017.

131 Ibid.

132 Ibid.

133 Ibid.

134 Loria, Kevin. "Armed police freed 11 tigers, 3 lions, and 3 bears from captivity - and that was just the beginning." *Business Insider*. BusinessInsider.com, 17 Mar. 2016. Web. 22 June 2017.

135 Ibid.

136 "Exotic Animal Incidents." *Born Free* . N.p., n.d. Web. 22 June 2017.

137 Ibid.

138 Ibid.

139 Ibid.

140 Ibid.

141 Ibid.

142 Ibid.

143 Ibid.

144 Ibid.

145 Ibid.

146 Ibid.

147 Ibid.

148 Ibid.

149 Ibid.

150 Ibid.

151 Ibid.

152 Ibid.

153 Feline Conservation Federation, 2016 Wild Feline Census.

154 Jauregui, Andres. "Leopard Shot, Killed by Indiana Man Did Not Belong To Wildlife Refuge." *The Huffington Post*. TheHuffingtonPost.com, 24 June 2013. Web. 22 June 2017.

Chapter 11

155 King, Robert C., and William D. Stansfield. *A Dictionary of Genetics*.

6th ed. New York: Oxford U Press, 2012. Print. Page 11

156 Ibid., 13

157 Ibid., 347

158 Ibid., 115

159 Ibid., 189

160 Ibid., 154

161 Ibid., 349

162 Ibid., 160

163 Ibid., 189

164 Ibid., 228

165 Ibid., 240

166 Ibid., 240

167 Ibid., 257

168 Ibid., 295

169 Ibid., 189

170 Ibid., 350

171 Schneider, Alexsandra, Corneliu Henegar, Kenneth Day, Devin Absher, Constanza Napolitano, Leandro Silveira, Victor A. David, Stephen J. O'Brien, Marilyn Menotti-Raymond, Gregory S. Barsh, and Eduardo Eizirik. "Recurrent Evolution of Melanism in South American Felids." *PLOS Genetics*. Public Library of Science, 19 Feb. 2015. Web. 22 June 2017.

172 Robinson, PhD, Tara Rodden. *Genetics for Dummies*. 2nd ed. Hoboken, NJ: Wiley Pub., 2010. Print. Page 187

173 Ibid., 188

174 Ibid., 189

175 Ibid., 197

176 Schneider, Alexsandra, Victor A. David, Warren E. Johnson, Stephen J. O'Brien, Gregory S. Barsh, Marilyn Menotti-Raymond, and Eduardo Eizirik. "How the Leopard Hides Its Spots: ASIP Mutations and Melanism in Wild Cats." *PLoS ONE*. Public Library of Science, 12

Dec. 2012. Web. 22 June 2017.

177 Kawanishi, K., M. E. Sunquist, E. Eizirik, A. J. Lynam, D. Ngoprasert, Wan Shahruddin W. N., D. M. Rayan, D. S. K. Sharma, and R. Steinmetz. "Near fixation of melanism in leopards of the Malay Peninsula." *Journal of Zoology*. Blackwell Publishing Ltd, 13 July 2010. Web. 22 June 2017.

178 Ibid.

179 "Punnett Square." *Punnett Square | Science Primer*. N.p., n.d. Web. 22 June 2017.

180 Ibid.

181 "Panther Fact Sheet." *World Animal Foundation*. N.p., n.d. Web. 22 June 2017.

182 Ibid.

183 "Mutant Leopards." *Messy Beast*. N.p., n.d. Web. 22 June 2017.

184 Arnold, Michael Lynn. *Natural hybridization and evolution*. New York: Oxford U Press, 1997. Print. Page 3

185 Ibid., 58

186 Ibid.

187 Ibid., 59

188 Ibid.

189 Ibid.

190 Ibid., 63

191 Ibid.

192 Ibid.

Chapter 12

193 Ford, Hope. "Family spots possible panther." *KLFY*. N.p., 05 July 2013. Web. 22 June 2017.

194 Ibid.

195 Miller, Shari. "Is this the Beast of Trowbridge? Couple catch 'puma-like creature' on film and claim they watched it catch and eat prey." *Daily Mail Online*. Associated Newspapers, 16 Aug. 2013. Web. 23 June 2017.

196 Ibid.

197 Mayes, Mike. "Black Panther Photographed in the Texas Hill Country?" *Texas Cryptid Hunter*. N.p., 15 Feb. 2012. Web. 22 June 2017.

Chapter 13

198 "Chasing Mpumalanga's Black Leopard." *ShowMe™ - Nelspruit*. N.p., 20 Mar. 2013. Web. 24 June 2017.

Chapter 15

199 Lewis, Chad, and Nick Redfern. *Hidden headlines of Texas: strange, unusual, & bizarre newspaper stories 1860-1910*. Eau Claire, WI: Unexplained Research Pub. Co., 2007. Print. Page 64.

200 Goode, G. Baron, and Professor S.P. Langley, comps. *Report of the United States National Museum, Under the Direction of the Smithsonian Institution, 1887*. Washington, D.C.: United States Government, 1889. Print. Pages 17 and 93.

Index

GENERAL

66th Infantry Division, 4
81st Infantry Division, 3, *4*
81st Regional Support Command, 3

Alabama and Coushatta Tribe, 8
Aztecs, *7,* 81

Born Free USA, 101, 103, 163

Carolina Panthers (NFL), 2
catamount, 2, 3, 66, 155
chromosome, 109
cougar, *viii,* xii, 1, 2, 3, 6, 7, 9, 24, 28, 33, 40, *41,* 55, 56, 57, 58, 60, 65, 66, 67, 68, 69, 70, 71, 72, 73, 74, 75, 92, 94, 102, 104, 110, 121, 126, 151, 155, 156, 157, 165, 168, 170, 175, 176, 182, 185, 190, 191, 194, 195, 196, 197
cougar noire, 70, *71, 74, 176*
coyotes, xiv, 14, 30, 43, 61, 80, 120, 140, 143, 155, 161
cryptid, xv, 5, 47
Feline Conservation Federation, 103, 104, 106
feral cat, 86, 87, 88, 89, 91, 92, 94, 161
Florida panther, 2, 9, 66, 119, 120, 160, 174, 176
Florida Panthers (NHL), 2

gene, 63, 109, 111, 157
 agouti, 109, 110, 111
 allele, 109, 111, 113, 114, 115, 116, 117, *118,* 119, 120, 169, 172, 175
 dominant, 63, 109, 113, 114, 115, 116, 117, 118, 119, 154, 169, 172, 174, 175
 recessive, 63, 109, 113, 114, 115, 116, 117, 118, 175
genotype, 109, 113, 114, 115, 117

heterozygous, 109, 113, 114, 115, 116, 117
Histoire Naturelle, 70, 176
homozygous, 109, 114, 115, 116, 117
Humane Society of the United States, 97
hybrid/hybridization, 119, 120, 121, 164, 166, 170, 172, 173, 174

jaguar, 3, *7,* 8, 26, 51, 52, 53, 54, 55, 56, 57, 58, 59, 60, 61, 62, 63, 66, 69, 70, 113, 119, 121, 129, 130, 151, 152, 153, 154, 158, 160, 162, 165, 166, 169, 170, 171, 172, 174,

175, 186, 197
jaguar warriors, 7
jaguarundi, 75, 76, 77, 79, 80, 81, 83, 84, 85, 94, 124, 127, 129, 131, 132, 133, 151, 158, 159, 161, 165, 166, 173, 174, 185, 187, 188, 195, 198

leopards, 57, 89, 91, 96, 98, 103, 105, 106, 107, 112, 117, 121, 129, 139, 144, 152, 162, 163
lion, 3, 97, 102, 119

Macho A, 61
Macho B, 61, 62, 153
melanin, 109
melanism, vi, 1, 7, 51, 56, 63, 82, 108, 109, 110, 111, 112, 113, 114, 116, 117, 118, 121, 149, 153, 154, 156, 157, 166, 169, 170, 172, 174, 175
Memphis Brooks Museum of Art, 12
Mexican lion, 3, 53, 55, 167
Mexican tiger, 3, 53
mountain lion, 2, 3, 16, 17, 29, 33, 39, 40, 53, 54, 59, 61, 65, 66, 74, 75, 96, 102, 119, 143, 149, 150, 152, 155, 156, 157, 166, 169, 172, 183, 186, 187, 191, 194, 198
mountain screamer, 66
mutation, 63, 73, 109, 110, 111, 121, 156,
  germ cell, 110
  somatic cell, 110

National Forest Service, 32
natural selection, 93, 111, 112, 113, 117, 121, 170, 175

painter, 66
puma, 2, 3, 40, 66, 70, *71,* 72, 91, 92, 151, 155, 156, 165, 168, 171, 175

Smithsonian Institution, 176

Teotihuacan, 7
Texas Parks and Wildlife Department, x, 10, 35, 57, 60, 65
Tezcatlipoca, 7
tiger, 66, 96, 97, 98, *100,* 101, 102, 103, 105, 119
tiger, 53, 54
United States Department of Agriculture (USDA), 101, 104, 150, 163
United States National Museum, 176

Wildcat, 3, 4, 8, 66, 75, 167
Wildlife Conservation Society (WCS), 41, 42
wolf, 120, 174
  gray, 120
  red, 120, 174

MEDIA

Dallas Morning News, 3
Donaldsonville Chief, 54

Galveston Daily News, 9
Galveston Tri-Weekly, 9
Galveston Weekly News, 9, 55

Houston Morning Star, 8
Houston Telegraph and Texas Register, 8
Huffington Post, 162

Journal of Zoology, 112

Kountze News, 69

London Daily Mail, 126

Melbourne Herald Sun, 94
Mobile Register, 83, *84*
Nelspruit News, 139

San Antonio Daily Light, 3, 167
San Antonio Express, 55
San Francisco Chronicle, 16, 19

Tetrapod Zoology, 90
Texas Cryptid Hunter, xiii, xv, 37, *38, 45, 46, 47,* 59, 77, *82, 84, 85, 123, 124, 127,* 128, 129, *130, 131, 132, 136,* 139, 183, 185, 190, 215

MAPS AND CHARTS

2016 Wild Feline Census, 104, 106

Average Annual Rainfall Map (Texas), 39, 45

Black Panther Sightings by County Chart (Texas), 49, 50
Black Panther Sightings by County Map (Texas), 45, 46, 47
Black Panther Sightings Distribution Map (Texas), 38

Major Rivers of Texas Map, 46

PEOPLE

Athreya, Vidya, 42
Atkinson, Bill, 90

Bindernagel, Dr. John, 34
Block, W.T., 8
Broaddus, Jim, 150, 151, 152, 153, 154, 155, 156, 157, 158, 159, 160, 162, 163, 164, 171, 175, 176, 179

Capparella, Dr. Angelo, vii, 16, 17, 18, 19
Chambers, Kevin, 103, 179
Cloar, Carroll, 12
Compte de Buffon, Georges Louis, 70, 71, 74, 176

Dobie, J. Frank, 11

Eason, I.C., 10, 11

Fleshman, Jim, 73
Fullingim, Archie, 69, 176

Gerhard, Ken, 19

Harcourt, Noel, 91

Jurek, Ron, 87

Lawson, John, 53, 54,
Lever, Christopher, 87
Liss, Cathy, 101

Martin, Howard, 8
McClurken, Mark, 141, 142, 143,
    144, 145, 146
Menkhorst, Peter, 92
Miller, Shari, 126
Moore, Chester, 127, 150, 151, 152,
    153, 154, 155, 156, 157, 158, 159,
    160, 161, 162, 163, 164, 165, 174,
    179

Nash, Darren, 90
Neill, Wilfred T., 81

Pennant, Thomas, 70, 74
Pittman, Blair, 10

Rebsamen, William, 12, 179
Redfern, Nick, 19
Rodrigues, Amy, 149, 150, 152,
    153, 154, 156, 157, 158, 159, 160,
    161, 162, 163, 164, 165, 177, 179
Rosatte, Rick, 55, 56, 57
Ruiz Herrero, Miguel, 71, 176

Shireman, Michelle, 149, 151, 152,
    153, 154, 155, 156, 157, 158, 159,
    160, 161, 162, 163, 164, 165, 179

Shuker, Dr. Karl, 118
Stewart, Jeff, 72, *90,* 135, 150, 151,
    152, 153, 154, 155, 156, 157, 158,
    159, 160, 161, 162, 163, 164, 165,
    173, 179

Thomson, William, 70, 74, 176
True, F.W., 176

Verrill, A. Hyatt, 81

Werner, Lisa, 150, 151, 152, 153,
    154, 155, 156, 157, 158, 159, 160,
    161, 162, 163, 164, 165, 171, 175,
    179
Wilder, Laura Ingalls, 67, 68, 69

PLACES

Alabama, 33, 82, 83, 84, 100, 104,
    160
   Montgomery, 101
Arkansas, 12, 33, 100, 104
   Eureka Springs, 102, 105
   Montgomery County, 11
Arizona, 61, 62, 63, 69, 80, 153
   Arizona Game and Fish
    Department, 61, *62*
   Cochise County, 62
   Douglas, 61
   Peloncillo Mountains, 61
   Prima County, 62
   Santa Cruz County, 62
   Tucson, 61, 153
Australia, 88, 89, 91, 92, 93, 124,
    161, 162, 173

Dunkeld, 91
Gippsland, 91, *92,* 93
Lara, 94
Victoria, 91, 92

Canada, 35, *65,* 66, 155, 157
 Ontario, xiii, 55, 56, 58
  Guelph, 56, *57*
  Ontario Ministry of Natural Resources, 55
California, xiii, 30, 39, 87
 Alameda County, 16
 California Department of Fish and Game, 87
 Dublin, 16
 Los Angeles, 39, 41
 San Ramon Hills, 16
 Santa Monica, 40
Central America, 7, 76, 81, 112, 158, 175
 Costa Rica, 71, 156, 176
  Guanacaste, 71

Florida, 2, 9, 33, 66, 80, 81, 97, 98, 100, 102, 104, 119, 155, 160, 171, 173
 Brevard County, 81
 Brooksville, 102
 Chiefland, 81
 Columbia County, 80
 Gulf Breeze, 102
 Ichetucknee River, 80
 Loxahatchee, 102, 103
 Marion County, 81
 Miami, 102
 Orange County, 80

Rock Springs, 80
Spring Hill, 101
Wellington, 102

Georgia, 33, 100, 104

Illinois, 40
 Chicago, 40, 155
India, 41, 42
Indiana, 107, 162,
 Charlestown, 106

Kentucky, 33, 100, 104
 Shepherdsville, 103

Louisiana, 33, 54, 100, 104, 125
 Ascension Parish, 54
 Fort Polk, 102
 Iberia Parish, 125

Malaysia, 112
 Isthmus of Kra, 112
 Malaysian Peninsula, 112
Mexico, 7, 35, 36, 55, 60, *62,* 63, 65, 76, 81, 112, 151, 153, 158, 175
Michigan, 126
 Lapeer County, 126
Mississippi, 33, 84, 85, 100, 104
Missouri, 40, 53
 Benton County, 53

New Mexico, *viii,* 62, 63, 153, 179
 Hidalgo County, 62
North Carolina, xiii, 16, 19, 31, 100
 Bath, 18

Bellhaven, 18
Cleveland County, 102
Fairfield, 18
Gaston County, 102
Hyde County, 17
Mattamuskeet, 17
Rose Bay, 18
Tyrrell County, 18
Washington, 18

Oklahoma, 33, 100, 104, *130*
  Oklahoma City, 101
  Ouachita Mountains, 130

South America, 70, 76, 112, 151, 153, 176
  Brazil, 70
    Carandahy River, 70
South Carolina, 53, 100, 132
  Columbia, 132

Tennessee, 12, 33, 100, 104, 155
Texas, xi, xiii, xiv, xvi, 1, 2, 3, 4, 6, 8, 9, 10, 11, 13, 14, 15, 18, 19, 20, 22, 23, 27, 31, 32, 33, 34, 35, 36, 37, 38, 39, *41,* 43, 44, 45, 46, 47, 48, 51, *52,* 54, 55, 58, 59, *62,* 63, 64, 65, 66, 69, 71, 72, 74, 75, 76, 77, 79, 80, 81, 82, 85, 87, 88, 90, 94, 96, 103, 104, 105, 107, 108, 112, 122, 123, 127, 134, 135m 137, 138, 139, 141, 145, 146, 147, 148, 150, 151, 152, 153, 154, 155, 158, 163, 164, 165, 168, 169, 170, 171, 172, 173, 174, 175, 176, 177, 179, 180, 215

Allen, 78
Alto, 20, 194
Angelina National Forest, 36
Arbor Hills Nature Preserve, 180, 196
Austin, *123,* 185
Barton Creek, 194
Big Thicket National Preserve, 8, 10, 19, 36, 37, 55, 69, 70, 176, 181
Bishop, 78
Bosque River, 80, 195
Brazoria, 26
Brazos River, 39, 45, 188
Bridgeport, 102
Burnet, 133, 185
Central Plains Region, 35, 36
Cleburne, 78
Colorado River, 192
Conroe, *100,* 101
Dallas, 39, 58, 69, 102, 131, 139, 140, 170
Danbury, 79
Davy Crockett National Forest, 36
Dawson, 6
Dayton, 194
Denton, 36, 39
El Paso, 40
Emory, 197
Falcon Lake, 58
Flat Fork Creek, 198
Fort Worth, 25, 36, 39, 183
Gonzales, 25, 26
Great Plains Region, 35, 36, 38
Gulf Coast Plains, 35

Hardin, 23,
Hill Country, 36, 38, 44, 65, 127, 168, 190
Hillsboro, 28, 183
Hooks, 25, 189
Horseshoe Bay, 134
Hull, 23
Huntsville, 140
Hurst, 27
Ingram, 102
Katy, 79, 194
Klein, 24, 184
Lake LBJ, 134
Lake Ray Hubbard, 131, 192
Laredo, 59
Lewisville, 79
Lingleville, 25
Liverpool, 80
Livingston, 15
Llano, 24, 129, 183
Lumberton, 9
Madisonville, 139, 141
McDade, 182
Mineral Wells, 180, 194
Moulton, 25
Mount Calm, 199
Mountains and Basins Region, 35
Neches River, 10
Nocona, 194
Pampa, 60
Paris, 26, 27
Pecos River, 39
Pilot Grove, 3
Quanah, 59, 60
Queen City, 196
Quitman, 181

Raintree Lake, 19
Rio Grande River, 39, 55, 59, 60, 65
Rocky Branch, 128
Sabinal River, 186, 187
Sabine National Forest, 36
Sabine River, 9, 54
Saginaw, 201
Salado, 24, 40
Sam Houston National Forest, 36, 66
San Antonio, 38, 44
San Bernard River, 26, 195
San Felipe, 188
Sierra Blanca, 25
Slocum, 20
Smithville, 184
Spring Creek, 200
Tenaha, 198
Trinity River, 25
Tyler, 190
Waco, 73, 80, 195
Warren, 19
Willow Creek, 200
Wills Point, 195

Virginia, 33, 100, 104

Index *221*

About the Author

MICHAEL MAYES is a Central Texas-based history teacher and coach who has had a lifelong interest in strange phenomenon and mystery animals. For the past 15 years, he has investigated sightings of both out-of-place known animals and those that may, or may not, exist. He has appeared on numerous internet podcasts and radio programs, including *Expanded Perspectives*, *Spaced Out Radio*, and *The Author's Lounge*, to discuss his research, as well as on an episode of *The Lowe Files* on the A&E network in the fall of 2017. Michael is the owner and writer of the *Texas Cryptid Hunter* website and author of the illustrated children's book, *Patty: A Sasquatch Story*.

Have you seen a black panther or other mystery animal? The author is always interested in hearing about encounters with out-of-place or mystery animals. Report your sighting by emailing Michael at Texascryptidhunter@yahoo.com.

www.ingramcontent.com/pod-product-compliance
Lightning Source LLC
Chambersburg PA
CBHW051046160426
43193CB00010B/1080